"Whether becoming a winr
advisor, Billy Peterson al
and compelling: you can a
must read."

MW01194127

— PAUL REILLY, CHAIRMAN AND CEO,
RAYMOND JAMES FINANCIAL SERVICES

"I have long respected and admired Billy Peterson as both a top financial planner and as a world-class family man. Billy knows about commitment, the necessary discipline to become wildly successful and to help guide others to financial success. Read his book *Harnessing Your Wealth* to capture your full potential."

— JEFFREY T. DOBYNS, CFP®, CLU, CHFC,
PRESIDENT, SOUTHWESTERN INVESTMENT GROUP

"Billy Peterson rides another winner...and this time it's a book. The former jockey's clear-headed optimism and grit in the face of constant obstacles is a story every investor can learn from."

— ROBERT A. ISBITTS, FOUNDER AND CHIEF INVESTMENT
STRATEGIST OF SUNGARDEN INVESTMENT MANAGEMENT

"Billy provides readers with an entertaining, no nonsense approach to starting, growing, and nurturing personal financial assets. Filled with anecdotes from Billy's firsthand experiences as a horse racing jockey, while in and out of the saddle (including some involuntary exits), or later as a competitive distance runner, he shares valuable lessons regarding the benefits of determination and discipline in an easy-to-understand format for anyone interested in learning about more effectively managing personal finances."

— SCOTT CURTIS, PCG PRESIDENT,
RAYMOND JAMES FINANCIAL SERVICES

Printed in the United States of America
First Printing, 2019

A hardcover edition of this book was published
in 2019 by Buck Way Press.

ISBN: 978-0-578-57422-6 (hardcover)
ISBN: 978-1-7340702-0-0 (paperback)
Library of Congress Control Number: 2019913565

Cover Design: Nanjar Tri Mukti
Interior Layout: Olivier Darbonville

https://www.petersonws.com/harnessing-your-wealth/

HARNESSING
— YOUR —
WEALTH

The Pursuit of
Millionaire
Status

BILLY PETERSON

Jay,
Thanks for your
support —
Best to you
and your
family!
Billy

FOREWORD

JaNae Francis

"The path to becoming a millionaire isn't just for the lucky. It's for you!"

— Billy Peterson

If we are to begin with the end in mind, I'd like to start off with telling you how Billy Peterson ends his book.

Billy not only ends this publication with these two sentences, he outlines how, given enough time, everyday people can become millionaires. And if you don't have years on your side, he's got advice for you too.

This publication is meant to show *everyone* how *they* could become a millionaire, not just the privileged and the fortunate.

This book, "Harnessing Your Wealth," is an interesting read on many levels. On the surface, this publication is a rags-to-riches tale of a boy who grew up facing some difficult circumstances who worked his way to success. Billy weaves his story with maturity, recognizing his launch to success originated in one of life's biggest challenges, a birth defect.

Success truly is for those who don't allow obstacles to stand in their way.

In this book, Billy successfully addresses a number of limiting beliefs, including:

"I'm too young."

An abundance of time is perhaps the greatest asset in Billy's formula for investing. There's not a time in one's life that's too early to start building wealth.

"I'm too old."

There are provisions in the law for those who are older than 50 to catch up to their desired retirement savings.

"I'm not enough."

Billy's life story alone is enough to inspire those who limit themselves with excuses to set them aside. I love how he started his first career as a jockey with nothing but confidence in himself and his own abilities. Confidence could improve just about anyone's lot in life.

"I'm not interested in money."

There are people who have learned to believe that gaining wealth makes one evil. Billy addresses this subject not only by showing how the wealthy have contributed to society but also how some have come to believe that money itself is bad.

"I don't have enough money."

Billy outlines how even a small investment can grow over time. Anyone can come up with $2,000 if they want to badly enough. He talks about youth who set out to mow lawns for their initial investments. He also shows how cutting back on unnecessary expenses can provide the funds they need to start investing.

"I may need my money for other things."

The stock market is a relatively liquid investment where funds can be sold any day the market is open. For this reason, investing in the stock market is more advisable than some other investments that are more difficult to cash out.

"The stock market is too volatile."

Confused by news coverage of an up-and-down stock market? In a story Billy wrote about two older men and their encounter with a successful investor, he offers an explanation of how individual companies can provide a solid investment foundation despite what the overall market is doing.

"The world is too unstable."

Billy not only shows how the stock market has recovered every time the market has experienced a downward turn but he also shows how investing when stocks are sold at cheaper prices is the easiest way to increase one's net worth.

"I'm too confused."

Admittedly, the stock market and other investments can be confusing for anyone, especially a beginner. Billy outlines the benefits of hiring a professional financial advisor in cutting through the confusion.

I found *"Harnessing Your Wealth"* by Billy Peterson to be an easy, fun read and outline for investing. I believe you will too.

ACKNOWLEDGMENTS

Writing a book isn't easy. It takes a great amount of time and motivation. I was inspired by several people who I would like to formally acknowledge here, but I also was aided in my lifetime in many other ways, and by many other people, which got me to this point in the first place.

I would like to thank my dad and my mom for raising me to be a responsible person and for always believing I could accomplish whatever I set out to do. Thank you both for showing me the value of hard work.

To Grandpa Peterson, I'll never forget how you treated me when I was just a lonely 12-year old boy with no friends and a broken family. You made me feel like I mattered.

I'd like to thank Shaun Peterson and Maggie Pigg for the great work you do each and every day. You guys are both super bright and intelligent and I enjoy the office environment you help create. You both step in whenever something is needed and have been instrumental in the success of Peterson Wealth Services as well as the Livastride Foundation. I'm so proud of the Financial Boot Camp and all the good things we do in our community. I also would like to thank everyone at Raymond James Financial Services for providing me with such a wonderful company with which to be affiliated.

To Mike Felter and Mike Monji, I haven't seen either of you in a long time and you probably don't realize it, but I consider you to be mentors in my careers. Your interest in my success was not taken for granted.

To all of the trainers and owners who trusted me to ride your horses, I hope you weren't disappointed in my effort. To my agents Raye Anne Holland and the late Monty Ohlemacher, you worked tirelessly on my behalf and believed in me when others didn't. Thank you for booking so many fantastic horses for me to ride to victory. It was truly a team effort.

To all of my clients, you should already know that I greatly value our relationship. My search for meaning was answered once I found I could help people like you make smart financial decisions that would enhance their quality of life.

Inspiration to write this book came from a company called Scribe Media. I attended a presentation by JT McCormick, the president of Scribe Media, at which he offered a free book written by co-founders Tucker Max and Zach Obront on how to write and publish your own book. I can't stress enough how important that book was for me to realize my words and my story mattered. I was able to find a starting point and get on track to make this book a reality. Thank you Scribe Media.

I also would like to thank my editors Debra Kastner and JaNae Francis for the fantastic work you did to get this book into published form. My cover designer Nanjar Tri Mukti and my interior designer Olivier Darbonville did outstanding work on producing a professional end product.

Others who assisted with the book include Steve Ozanich, Molly Hardy, Robert Isbitts and my internal compliance officer, Matthew Gourgues. Thank you all.

It is essential that I give credit to the man who taught me what investing was all about back when I was a 14-year-old boy, Mr. Kenny Tucker. I'll be forever grateful to you for taking the time necessary to teach a young man the value of investing for the long term. May you rest in peace.

I thank God for giving me so many blessings and for watching over me through countless riding accidents. Your patience, wisdom and guidance are the foundation for everything in my life.

And finally, I don't know where I'd be without the love and support of my wife Heather. You have taught me so much about life and the true meaning of happiness. You are my best friend and most trusted ally. I am so grateful to you for helping me push through, casting light on the power of the mind. Your spirit is eternally tied to mine.

To my children,

Cade, Karly, Kaiya, Brigham and Berkley.

You give me hope for tomorrow!

CONTENTS

The world owes you nothing. It was here first.

MARK TWAIN

INTRODUCTION

Since retiring from the racetrack after nine years as a professional jockey, I've worked in the financial industry for over 23 years with three different firms. I started in 1996 with PaineWebber in Long Beach, California and became a Senior Vice President of Investments. In 1999 I joined Smith Barney where I was named Senior Vice President of Wealth Management and led a team of five. In 2009, I felt that I would have better ability to serve my clients as an independent branch owner, so I took up affiliation with Raymond James Financial Services and now I am the president and owner of my own company and a five-time member of Raymond James Chairman's Council.[1] I have been named to Barron's list of top advisors[2] and selected to America's Best-in-State financial advisors by Forbes.[3]

In my nine years as a jockey, I won more than 1,000 races riding at notable racetracks in over a dozen states. I was recognized as the leading rider at multiple race meets and was the number one Quarter Horse jockey in the country in 1995. I've had a lot of success in both of my careers — earned, never given.

What I've learned in all my years of observing people is success doesn't come without effort. You must work hard to reach your career goals and accomplish personal achievements. On the other hand, successful investing isn't as difficult as most people make it out to be. With some discipline and the proper tools, you can change the course of your life in a dramatic way. In this book, I will show you how.

Tomorrow is the most important thing in life. Comes into us at midnight very clean. It's perfect when it arrives and it puts itself in our hands. It hopes we've learned something from yesterday.

JOHN WAYNE

[3] **Forbes Best-In-State Wealth Advisors, (2019).** The Forbes ranking of Best-In-State Wealth Advisors, developed by SHOOK Research, is based on an algorithm of qualitative criteria and quantitative data. Those advisors who are considered have a minimum of seven years of experience, and the algorithm weighs factors like revenue trends, AUM, compliance records, industry experience and those who encompass best practices in their practices and approach to working with clients. Portfolio performance is not a criteria due to varying client objectives and lack of audited data. Out of 29,334 advisors nominated by their firms, 3,477 received the award. This ranking is not indicative of an advisor's future performance, is not an endorsement, and may not be representative of an individual client's experience. Neither Raymond James nor any of its financial advisors or RIA firms pay a fee in exchange for this award/rating. Raymond James is not affiliated with Forbes or Shook Research, LLC.

Always drink upstream from the herd.

COWBOY WISDOM

CHAPTER ONE

FOLLOWING THE HERD

C hildren are influenced by their parents, who were influenced by *their* parents, and so forth. Decisions about careers, relationships, nutrition, lifestyle and yes, money, are all shaped by what we see from those closest to us. Even if what we witness is not the ideal or preferred route, we nonetheless find ourselves tracking many of the same habits as our parents.

Breaking out of bad practices is not all that hard to do. We simply need to stop for a moment, and take notice of these, almost unconscious, patterns. Oftentimes, the simple act of questioning certain behaviors can lead us into a new mindset, which will give us the motivation to cut loose from unproductive or unhealthy routines. We are talking about money habits in this book and the crisis facing our youth in that trillions of dollars of debt will need to be repaid to the U.S. Treasury at some point in the future. The repayment will likely come from a reduction in government assistance programs as well as an increase in the taxes collected from incomes and consumer purchases.

It's high time we all started to take our financial well-being more seriously so we won't be as affected by government decisions down the road.

STRIKE YOUR OWN PATH

What is success? What is wealth?

For some, they are one and the same. For others, they are miles apart. I enjoy asking these questions to all sorts of people in my daily work as a financial advisor and investment professional. The answers vary widely. The questions often catch people off guard. I have learned that most people have never even considered these questions before and are typically content to slide through life as if they were on an amusement park ride and they are simply passengers unable to alter their course.

What does success mean to you?

Can you verbalize it? Does it change each passing season or does it stay fairly constant?

If you can come up with a good definition of what success means for you and have a measurable plan to get there, then I believe you are on the path to achieving it. However, the path will not be without obstacles and hidden roots trying to trip you up. Focus and effort are necessary components necessary to accomplish any worthwhile goal.

Success can be small or large. It can be a lifelong pursuit or a daily checklist. For me, how I define success has changed over the years. Life tends to give and take from us constantly. Going through tough times, tragedies and despair gives us new perspectives on our lives.

To be fair, many will refer to success in terms of relationships as they ponder their family values. Such answers may include raising kids, seeing them go to college, or being married for 40 years, etc.

Those who set sights on achievement alone will continuously raise the bar after each accomplishment and soon find themselves unfulfilled on a seemingly never-ending treadmill on their climb to the top.

Finding peace within can and should be a cornerstone for living a successful life. The trick is in finding how to be settled with what you have and not always be looking over the fence for something else that catches your eye.

Isn't it nice to *not* want for things? Wouldn't life be easier if we didn't have to constantly worry about the next paycheck? We live in abundance when we are truly at peace with life as it is and are not at the mercy of external forces, including money.

This is what many refer to as *wealth*. Where does wealth fit in with your core values?

Sometimes people say, "I want to be rich." But what does that mean? The simple difference between a **rich** person and a **wealthy** person is that a **wealthy** person has sustainable wealth. In other words, a wealthy person will always be wealthy, whereas someone who is merely **rich** will only be so for a short period of time until the money is gone. **Rich** people only have money or possessions and not that which money ultimately provides, which I call prosperity. **Prosperity** is the long-term state of flourishing, thriving, good fortune or successful social status.

The majority of Americans aren't prosperous, and they are nowhere near being wealthy. Since they've never learned financial literacy and therefore do not understand the importance of planning and investing, they fall to the mercy of government assistance to support their way of life. Programs such as Social Security, food stamps, unemployment, Medicaid and federal housing, to name a few, are therefore huge drains on taxpayers in general.

To be clear, we should do our part to help those in need. My point is, too many people are faced with financial hardship which requires increased tax revenues to meet the burden. While on the surface government assistance appears quite harmless, too much leads to deficits, recessions and economic instability.

A former queen of England once said, "There are two types of people in this world – those willing to work and those willing to let them."

In our country, workers earn wages and pay taxes, which in turn provides resources necessary to fund the many aid and assistance programs. Programs such as Social Security were established by the government as a means to help people set aside money for their own retirement. The federal government began accepting a percentage of each person's wages from company payrolls as a safekeeping mechanism. The plan was to give back those funds to the wage earner beginning at retirement age and pay them out gradually each month until the person died.

Ideally, it would be like a forced savings plan where everyone had a private bank account and then could draw on those dollars to help them in retirement years. But the government isn't known for doing things efficiently. The program essentially evolved into a general pool of wage earners' money to be used to fund *all* retirement benefits, but relied upon wage earners' deposits to produce the payouts for those entering or in retirement. As age demographics shifted, the number of retirees began climbing in relation to the number of employed people. This imbalance has caused several modifications related to the ability to access our money, such as increasing the age considered normal retirement. Beyond 2019, we are facing the real risk of our *own* money not being available to us for our *own* retirement.

Crazy right?

They pull money out of our paychecks to hold for us because too many Americans are incapable of managing their own affairs, yet the pool of money will be dried up in less than 16 years, according to the Committee for a Responsible Federal Budget.[4] To continue paying out to retirees, the Social Security Administration will have to cut monthly benefits by 20-25 percent. Members of Congress won't touch the problem for fear of alienating many voters and costing them reelection. The problem is very real, but as mentioned, is not being addressed. The piper will need to be paid sooner or later, and I for one don't want to be at the mercy of what the government decides to do. Relying on others is never a comfortable situation. It has been my goal to help people gain more control with respect to their own financial destiny.

Ninety percent of the politicians give the other ten percent a bad reputation.

HENRY KISSINGER

The most common answer I get when asking, "What does wealth mean to you?" is *peace of mind.* The next most common is *financial freedom.* The younger generation, dubbed Generation Z, grew up in the age of media streaming, high-speed data transmission, smartphones, and artificial intelligence. They have been raised during a period of real estate and banking collapses, high profile Ponzi schemes and a general distrust of the Wall Street image. Many of these individuals

---

[4] "Analysis of the 2018 Social Security Trustees' Report." *Committee for a Responsible Federal Budget,* 19 June 2018, http://www.crfb.org/papers/analysis-2018-social-security-trustees-report.

born between the mid 1990's to 2010 have come to despise so-called wealthy individuals. Greed and corruption are partly to blame, but I also believe that a sense of (forgive me here) *entitlement* may be a root cause of the resistive mindset.

Somewhere along the way, kids, as a general population, came to expect their parents to do almost everything for them. Many of us have witnessed art work, school projects, fundraisers and various other responsibilities which were assigned to students, but were actually completed by the parents. By not being held accountable in this way, children don't learn how to deal with setbacks or life's inevitable struggles. Some parents think they're doing their children a great favor, but in reality, they are inflicting more harm on them than they could possibly realize. This damage will stay with them for many years – and sometimes, for life.

Kids need to fail! And they need to learn that it's OK to fail. Yes, failure is a critical component in the transformation to adulthood. Becoming a successful adult requires perseverance and commitment. As a high school coach, I observe athletes and their parents' involvement nearly every day. I have a pretty good idea as to which young adults are going to thrive after high school and which are going to struggle.

Parents want so badly for their children to succeed, they put the blinders on as to the abilities of their child compared to the others on the team. When playing time is impacted, instead of working harder, these kids become bitter and sour toward the coaches and the other players. As kids grow up, graduate high school and move into the world of jobs, families and responsibilities, they are ill-equipped. It's similar to a person entering a marathon without ever having run a single mile in preparation. Logically, when these young adults begin to fail with their jobs, marriages, bills and schedules they look for someone to blame. They also show resentment toward those who appear to be flourishing.

To justify their own unfortunate circumstances, they can easily fall into the mindset that having money is equivalent to corruption and greed.

And they want nothing to do with that.

I would like to take a stab at refuting the argument that wealth is evil. Take for example, Bill Gates – arguably one of the most *successful* (there's that term again) businessmen in U.S. history. He came from an affluent family, considering his father was a lawyer and was able to send him and his siblings to prestigious universities. Bill didn't believe Harvard could offer him much, however, so he dropped out in order to focus more on his main passion – computers, and later founded Microsoft. The rest is history.

Today, Bill and his wife, Melinda, rank among the wealthiest people in the world. The couple has already pledged more than $35 billion to charitable causes, mainly through their private foundation. This is remarkable as it represents approximately 40 percent of their total net worth.[5] Admittedly most of the charitable giving will occur after their passing, but the spirit of donating to important causes is admirable. In 2017, Gates invested $50 million into Alzheimer's research. Bill and Melinda have established programs to promote education both here and abroad and also have funded programs to provide much needed medical care to citizens of poorer countries. In 2010, they created *The Giving Pledge*, which is an initiative directed toward the ultra-wealthy, encouraging them to give at least half of their fortunes to charity. *The Giving Pledge* is a simple concept and one that attempts to hold the super wealthy accountable to the greater

---

[5] Kirsch, Noah. "Bill Gates' Net Worth Eclipses $100 Billion." *Forbes*, Forbes Magazine, 18 Apr. 2019, https://www.forbes.com/sites/noahkirsch/2019/04/18/bill-gates-net-worth-eclipses-100-billion-again/#dbc7852480e1.

good. It is an open invitation for billionaires, or those who would be if not for their giving, to publicly dedicate the majority of their wealth to philanthropy. To date, nearly 200 people have signed on.

We make a living by what we get;
we make a life by what we give.

WINSTON CHURCHILL

Ultimately, wealth is what you want it to be. If you *have* it, you can do whatever you want *with* it. You can help your more unfortunate family members pay off their mortgage or fund the new baseball field in your town. Maybe you'll decide to help build the new research center at the local hospital.

Wealth also allows you to avoid needing handouts from others, because you have essentially built your own garden or apple orchard which, if managed properly, will provide a lifetime of harvest. Thus, you won't need to turn to family, friends, or institutions for financial aid.

The largest source of financial aid in our country is the U.S. Treasury. Why care? Take the current U.S. national debt, for example, sitting at $22.3 trillion as of late April 2019 and climbing. At this time, there is no real solution to this massive problem being seriously discussed in Congress. Our country is literally in debt up to its eyeballs. And entitlement programs make up a significant portion of the annual additions to the debt level.

Medicare and Medicaid were created to assist older individuals with growing healthcare costs yet those costs have greatly exceeded what was originally estimated at their inception. The largest component of Medicaid is managed care, such as Hospice, followed by long-term care, both of which are typically end-of-life issues.

Medicaid is the nation's public health insurance program for people with low income. The Medicaid program covers one-in-five low-income Americans, including many with complex and costly needs for care.[6] Medicaid plays a critical role in covering certain demographic groups in child birth and with disabilities. The program is the principal source of long-term care coverage for Americans with few or no assets. Money for these programs comes from state and national funds and is the third-largest domestic program in the federal budget, after Social Security and Medicare. It is the second-largest component of state budgets only behind education.

I should make it very clear that just as meat doesn't grow in supermarkets, state and national assistance programs don't come from money trees. Those programs are fed from tax revenues paid by the American taxpayer.

Back in the old west, when folks had to pull up their own pants, there was no such thing as waiting for a welfare check or disability check to arrive. I'd guess there were many significant physical hardships admirably lived out in those days. Many people today are receiving full government disability payments with far fewer adversities. I have personally witnessed several so-called *disabled* people playing golf, tennis or water sports and yet they continue to milk the system for a free handout.

The only problem is, this handout is not really free. The burden falls on the people. People like you and me. This isn't to say that many millions of people don't have serious or severe disabilities. They

---

[6] Rudowitz, Robin, et al. "10 Things to Know about Medicaid: Setting the Facts Straight." *The Henry J. Kaiser Family Foundation,* 6 Mar. 2019, https://www.kff.org/medicaid/issue-brief/10-things-to-know-about-medicaid-setting-the-facts-straight/.

absolutely do and they rely on the financial assistance that government programs or charitable organizations provide. I serve on the board for the Permanently Disabled Jockeys Fund (PDJF) and I see firsthand how essential it is to assist those who must deal with heavy physical burdens. This is yet another way wealth can be put to good use.

When we think about paying taxes, we typically want to believe our dollars paid into the federal, state and local governments are going to be used in the best way possible, to provide the biggest benefit to the most number of people. I think we all want an honest system which provides for necessities, such as roads, bridges, hospitals, law enforcement and schools. Additionally we need to maintain a solid defense program to protect our citizens and way of life. Finally, we need to help those who are less fortunate via certain entitlement programs. All of these *needs* require funding. You may be curious as to how much tax revenue is generated by the different income levels. From data taken in 2016, the top 50 percent of all taxpayers paid 97 percent of all individual income taxes, while the bottom 50 percent paid the remaining 3 percent. The top 1 percent – or super high-income earners – paid more than 37 percent of all income taxes in 2016.[7]

Aspiring to become wealthy is not a sin. Financial aid to the less fortunate is largely paid for by those with higher incomes. I believe youth should actually set goals for themselves to reach financial independence, because with those achievements comes more economic growth, less reliance on government assistance and a happier lifestyle. Studies have shown that wealth makes us happier when it's earned, not given. Proof of this concept is everywhere. Think about the proverbial *Trust Fund Baby*. What image does that term conjure up

---

[7] Bellafiore, Robert. "Summary of the Latest Federal Income Tax Data, 2018 Update." *Tax Foundation*, 22 Aug. 2019, https://taxfoundation.org/summary-latest-federal-income-tax-data-2018-update/.

for you? True happiness or the empty pursuit of happiness? How about the lottery winners who receive instant riches? It's easy to say that hitting the lottery would be the ultimate source of joy and solve all of our problems. However, most lottery winners are miserable with their new circumstances within only a few short years after the windfall.

Easy come and easy go.

I was a professional athlete for nearly a decade. I can assure you that athletes are some of the worst protectors of wealth on the planet. High-dollar athletes are well known for doing amazing things on the field of play – actions most humans can only dream of doing. Yet with their finances, they make one error after another. They are typically young and uneducated as to the importance of spending within their means. They make large sums of money but they usually aren't able to peer into the future far enough to realize that the income they receive to perform a sport or play a game will someday end. Often, the end comes abruptly due to injury or failure to perform at the level necessary to remain on the team payroll, or to garner mounts as in professional horse racing. According to a study done by Sports Illustrated, 80 percent of NFL players are bankrupt within two years of retirement, and 60 percent of NBA players are bankrupt within five years of retirement.[8] Some of this is self-sabotage in that athletes want to project a certain image, so they purchase fancy cars and homes and always have an entourage of hangers-on who like to claim they are part of the inner circle of any particular highly recognizable athlete. Mike Tyson went through nearly $300 million, which was his estimated net worth back in his glory days. Today, he has an approximate net worth of $3 million.

---

[8] "Personal Finances of Professional American Athletes." *Wikipedia*, Wikimedia Foundation, 29 July 2019, https://en.wikipedia.org/wiki/Personal_finances_of_professional_American_athletes.

Interestingly, those who have to fight the hardest to reach the top have a better likelihood of keeping what they get. In Quarter Horse racing, the All-American futurity is the pinnacle of the sport. I'd dreamed of riding in that race since the very first time I mounted a racehorse. In 1994, there were nearly 200 horses entered for the time trials, all attempting to post a fast enough time to qualify for the final gate, which would be run two weeks later. I qualified a horse named Doo Dominate as one of the 10 finalists and became one of the youngest jockeys to ever do so. The All-American is a $2 million futurity with the winner taking home more than $1 million. The build-up was intense. Film crews from ESPN and other major networks were on hand when the day finally arrived. Unfortunately, a bad moon was rising for me and Doo Dominate.

SET-BACKS ARE A PART OF LIFE

I felt something was off with Doo Dominate in the pre-race warmup. He didn't act as if his senses were firing. He wasn't *right*. Little did I know that he'd suffered a hair-line fracture in his right knee in a previous race and had done further damage to it during the time trials. The trainer had not said a thing about the horse being injured. He was only thinking of the million-dollar payoff. Three hundred yards into the 440-yard All-American, Doo Dominate's knee couldn't go any further and it snapped in half. The trainer had illegally blocked the horse's nerves in the front legs so the horse wouldn't feel anything. The horse literally ran himself into the ground. When the right knee broke going 45 mph, we had no chance of staying upright. He went down hard and threw me into the dirt like a slingshot. My years of rodeoing taught me how to come off of a horse. I instinctively tucked and rolled to my right.

30

This allowed me to avoid the impact directly to my neck and spine. By the grace of God, I walked off the track under my own will power. Doo Dominate wasn't so fortunate. This type of injury is life-ending for the horse – nothing can be done to repair a broken leg because a horse won't stay off the injured limb long enough for it to heal. It also is very often life-ending for the jockey as well. The force of the collision with the ground often snaps all sorts of bones, including the neck. One of my good friends and fellow riders, Sam Thompson, was killed this way in 2008. Sam died on Christmas Day at age 36. He was a great jockey and an even better person. The dangers are real!

In the aftermath of the 1994 All-American Futurity, especially due to its high profile and media attention, racing officials completed an in-depth investigation and determined that the trainer and owner of Doo Dominate had concealed the horse's injuries and jeopardized lives in choosing to run the horse. They were banned from ever racing in the country again.

Losers quit when they fail. Winners fail until they succeed.

ROBERT T. KIYOSAKI

I took a long time to overcome that tragedy. It haunted me and caused me to suffer from PTSD, although I didn't have a doctor officially diagnose me. I was a jockey and riding racehorses was what I did. I had to get back in the saddle. Each horse I rode brought new fears that hadn't been there before. For the first time in my career, I was scared of getting hurt.

For a jockey, fear equals demise. You can't win if you're afraid and if you go long enough without winning, your career is over. My pride wouldn't let me give up. Not that way. I was determined to overcome those fears, and within a few months, I had climbed to the top of the jockey standings once again, although I wasn't sure if I would get another shot at the All-American.

I know that fear is an obstacle for some people,
but for me it is just an illusion... Failure always makes me
try harder on the next opportunity.

MICHAEL JORDAN

MAKE YOUR OPPORTUNITIES COUNT

As fate would have it, I found my saving grace in a horse named Winalota Cash. He was a 2-year-old in 1995 and was the fastest horse I had ever ridden – one of the fastest to ever step on a racetrack. We won the 1995 All-American in race record time, besting the times of all 36 prior winners since the race incepted in 1959. It was a story of tragedy to triumph. I had achieved my dream and it provided me with many more opportunities as a jockey. (Winalota Cash would be named World Champion that year - a rare feat for a 2-year-old - after finishing the season with more than $1.5 million in earnings.)

My share of the purse winnings was about $100,000, all for a 21.14-second ride. What did I do with all of that money? I paid my agent 20 percent, my valet 2 percent, gave $23,000 to my in-laws, as they were going through bankruptcy due to a failed business, set aside $25,000 for taxes and I contributed the rest into a SEP-IRA in which I purchased some growth stock funds. That provided me with a sizable tax deduction on the earnings and also boosted my retirement funding plan. Today, that $19,500 contribution is worth a significant amount, and I have continued adding money to various retirement plans every year since. What I *didn't* do was piss any of the money away on unnecessary items.

I rode with dozens of high-profile jockeys who would be considered celebrities in the horse racing world. I watched them and idolized them for years as they won big races and appeared in magazines and on television. I can count only about five of them who were smart with their earnings and were able to retire comfortably from the sport. The majority of them had to retire due to age, injuries, or necessity because of lack of opportunities.

A friend of mine who won his share of big races quipped, "The trainers retired me quite a few years ago. I just didn't realize it at the time." What he meant was that over the years, he received fewer and fewer riding requests from trainers and his income dropped steadily, yet he remained in the sport because he didn't have a backup plan. He couldn't walk away with dignity and only quit years later out of pure necessity in order to provide a reasonable income for his family. Instead of having a comfortable retirement, ex-jockeys often become racing officials, track maintenance workers, valets or agents for other jockeys. In the end, they retire to other lower-paying jobs. I estimated the average jockey burns through more than $5 million during a 20-year career.

Sooner or later, we all face the reality that we can no longer do the work we once could. Toby Keith sums it up this way, "I'm not as good as I once was, but I'm as good *once*, as I ever was." Long before that day comes, we need to have a plan for how to deal with it. The expenses of life don't just stop once we retire or lose our job to a more productive replacement. Spending money can become an addiction. For some people, buying new things is their only form of happiness. The trouble is, the happiness is short-lived and at the expense of sustainable wealth.

Home is where you keep your stuff
while you are out buying more stuff.

GEORGE CARLIN

Building wealth is one thing, keeping it is another. You can do it, however, just as I did and many others have done. In this book, I'll show you the path and lay out the ribbons along the way so you don't accidentally take a wrong turn. The important thing to remember before we dive in is that this requires some effort on your part. Not much, but some.

"Nothing happens until somebody does something." One of my professors in college used to say that all the time. What will you choose to do? I'm about to share with you a roadmap which has allowed many people to become wealthy. You can also make this happen for yourself. The only thing standing in your way is one tiny word – action.

The first step in getting somewhere is deciding
you're not going to stay where you are.

CHAUNCEY DEPEW

It's hard to beat a guy when he's got his mind made up he's going to win.

MUHAMMAD ALI

CHAPTER TWO

CHANGING YOUR MINDSET

E very fall, my staff and I host a financial literacy boot camp at Weber State University. The idea blossomed in 2006 after reading an article stating that young adults were ill equipped for the financial decisions facing them in the real world. My staff and I came up with the idea to teach financial concepts to teens in a one-day boot camp format. It took a few years, but in 2010, we finally got the project underway. The first year, we hosted about 20 kids, then 40 the year after. By the third year, we hosted more than 200 and now we cap it at 600 students.

Local high schools make it a field trip for their junior and senior financial literacy students and they bus them up to the university for the full-day event. We hold breakout sessions to cover debt management, investing concepts, retirement and employee benefit plans, and preparing for life after high school.

WILL YOU BECOME A MILLIONAIRE?

During the investing segment, I ask the class to raise their hands if they believe they will become a millionaire someday. Typically, about half the class keeps their hands down. Then I go on the offense. I ask students directly *why* they don't believe they will become millionaires.

Answers are predictable, "I don't plan to pursue a career that pays much money."

"What career are you planning to pursue?" I ask.

Usually the response is along the lines of a teacher, physical therapist, construction worker, etc. (I currently represent clients in all of those careers who are millionaires.) Other students will say they don't have any way to invest money because their family is poor or they are in debt paying for credit cards or a car and just have to get by.

I also hear the resigned, yet stoic answer, "I don't want to be a millionaire."

I follow up on this one. "Why not?"

"Well, money just doesn't seem all that important to me."

This one is harder to debate, but I do anyway.

"I understand money is not the answer to everything, but I also understand that it provides comfort and freedom to pursue life in a more untethered way." I encourage students to stop clinging to the belief that getting wealthy is only for the lucky or fortunate souls who catch a break. Becoming wealthy is a possibility for everyone, no matter where they came from or what dire situations befell them early in life.

I have a long-time friend named Juan who I first met when I was 19 years old and riding first call for a highly successful trainer named Lee Giles. Juan had become a very successful business owner all through sheer tenacity and determination, which allowed him to pursue fun activities such as horse racing. Lee had become the leading trainer in the intermountain area through years of hard work. He came from humble beginnings on a farm with a very large family, all growing up in a tiny house out in the middle of nowhere, a place called Tabiona, Utah.

Juan had it somewhat tougher. He'd flown to the United States from Spain, where he'd grown up in near poverty on a small farm. When he was a teenager, he'd obtained a work visa for the United States to work in the agricultural industry. He had heard of a few other Spaniards who'd moved here to work as sheepherders. Juan lined up a job with a sheep rancher in Idaho, who purchased a one-way ticket for him. He flew direct to New York's Kennedy airport, unable to speak a word of English. He didn't know how to navigate an airport, nor how to read the monitors to catch his connection flight to Denver and then on to Boise. Luckily, he happened to come across an old Catholic priest who spoke a few words of Basque and who also was traveling on the Denver connection. The priest made sure Juan found his flight and wished him well. He made it to Boise at 2:30 in the morning, hungry and alone. Eventually, that morning, he was picked up by the rancher and driven up into a mountain range far away from civilization. There he was given a rifle, a few bags of groceries, two herding dogs, an old horse and a small tent to sleep in. He was placed in charge of 1,700 head of sheep.

The foreman would come around to check on him every two weeks, bringing some food and other supplies. He had offered Juan $10 cash or a gallon of wine for every bear he killed. One summer he killed 11 bears, which were constantly attacking his sheep. He chose the wine in every case. He was only 18 and as lonely as he could be.

Life went on like this for several years, until one day, after he was awarded his green card, he was offered an opportunity in town to become a welder. It was just an instructional program but nonetheless, he dedicated himself to learning to weld and eventually became so good at it that he decided to start his own company. Over time, Juan's company was awarded tens of millions of dollars in contracts doing highly technical jobs inside of power plant boilers and mining facilities. He would ultimately sell his business for a lot of money and retire to live on a farm raising horses, chickens and crops with his wife, Diane. He wasn't afraid to take the risk, and when he was given the opportunity to pull himself up, he grabbed the rope and climbed his way to the top.

According to Christian teachings, the seven deadly sins are *pride, greed, lust, envy, gluttony, wrath, and sloth.*

In my book, *victimhood* is another deadly sin.

Don't sell yourself short. Countless people have overcome extreme hardships, such as poverty, physical handicaps, abandonment, abuse, and other terrible circumstances to make a positive difference in the world by becoming very wealthy and then giving back to those causes about which they are passionate.

Oprah Winfrey didn't have wealth handed to her. She was born into poverty in rural Mississippi to a teenage, single mother and was later raised in an inner-city neighborhood. She's acknowledged that she had been raped at the very early age of 9 and became pregnant at age 14. This resulted in a son who would later die as an infant. This woman could easily have folded. She could have accepted that life was not worth living, or at least not worth putting much effort into.

But she didn't. She made the decision to reach higher and ask for more. She now is one of America's greatest success stories and has a net worth in excess of $2.6 billion, according to Forbes.

Tom Cruise grew up in a poor household – near the poverty level. He and his siblings were abused by a dominating father. He was beaten by his dad, whom Cruise stated was a bully and a coward. "He was the kind of person where, if something went wrong, they kick you. It was a great lesson in my life – how he'd lull you in, make you feel safe and then bang! For me, it was like 'There's something wrong with this guy. Don't trust him and be careful around him.'"[9] Overcoming that childhood must have been difficult. Neglect and emotional abuse are bad enough, but when you throw in physical abuse, there is often permanent, psychological damage. Tom found his way and kept to his long-term dream. He has been nominated for three Academy Awards and has won three Golden Globes. In 2012, Cruise was the highest-paid actor in Hollywood and in 2017, he was ranked third with $43 million in earnings.

These are a couple of examples of very notable people who overcame significant troubles and hardships to reach their goals. The world is full of stories such as these and I find them very inspiring. I like to read autobiographies of people with great stories to tell. We can learn to find the inner strength, the will to persevere, and the mental toughness to keep getting back on the horse after getting thrown. Your career largely depends on how much work you put into it.

What will you do with your life?

The Harder I Work, the Luckier I get

SAMUEL GOLDWYN

---

[9] Spodek, Joshua. "12 Incredibly Successful People Who Overcame Adversity." *Inc.com*, Inc., 20 May 2016, https://www.inc.com/joshua-spodek/12-incredible-people-who-succeeded-despite-adversity.html.

DETERMINE YOUR OWN FATE

To provide some context about overcoming life's obstacles, I'm going to share a condensed version of my upbringing. This is not meant to make anyone feel sorry for me, nor is it to dwell on my own difficulties. I share this to illustrate that where there is a will, there is a way.

My childhood was filled with some of the typical good stuff, such as big family Christmas parties, Easter picnics, playing all sports and riding my horses. There was a short trip to Disneyland when I was five and a few fond memories of going to the movies and learning to ride my bike.

Mostly, though, I remember the bad stuff. I remember the months I spent at age 3 in Shriners Hospital wondering why my parents had left me there and not knowing what was wrong with me. My mom did visit me, but I was so scared and so sad that I mostly just remember her leaving, over and over again. I was placed in a ward with several other children. One boy had no arms and I remember him pushing me in my wheelchair, using nothing but his chest. Another boy was so severely burned on his upper body and face that I couldn't tell if he was smiling or crying. I was in there waiting to have corrective leg surgery because I was born with severely bowed legs. My parents didn't have insurance to cover a surgery at the children's hospital so they opted for Shriner's – the charitably-run hospital for kids in bad shape but unable to afford the medical treatments.

Back then, the only known treatment that provided some level of correction to the condition was cutting the femur bones, rotating them slightly inward and stapling them back together. The bowing is a genetic condition in our family known as X-linked Hypo-Phosphotemia, also known as Ricketts. It had been passed down from my maternal grandfather to my mother and then to me. The boys in the family are physically affected by the condition. Several of my cousins have the trait. The women are carriers but they don't display the condition themselves. I will pass this to my daughters and they will pass it to their sons and so on. My son has perfectly straight legs, as do my daughters, although the girls carry it genetically and have a 50 percent chance of passing that X chromosome to their sons.

After quite a long stay at Shriners just waiting, my turn for a surgeon to become available finally came and my surgery was done. I went home in a full-body cast from feet to chest to recover, although I would need to endure several more surgeries before it was over. Today, I still have pretty significant bowing. People assume it's because I spent so many years riding horses. I just agree and change the subject. Now, we have a clearer understanding of what causes the legs to bow. Those born with the deficiency can be treated with a potent combination of Vitamin D and Phosphorous and their legs straighten right up.

Being born with bowed legs was part of my destiny. We have to play the cards we're dealt. By cutting my femur bones and making the rotation to each leg, my growth was stunted. My family members are all quite tall. Doctors have told me that without the surgery, I would have reached 5'11" or maybe even 6 feet. Without the Ricketts, I would have experienced a much different life.

As it turned out, I hit my maximum height at 5'6" – and as fate would have it, my short stature enabled me to pursue a career as a jockey. I was able to ride at tracks such as Santa Anita, Hollywood Park, Delmar, Bay Meadows, Ruidoso Downs, Remington Park, and Sunland Park, to name a few – riding some of the most highly-accomplished racehorses in the country. I would later become the No. 1 ranked Quarter Horse jockey across the globe in 1995.[10]

---

[10] AQHA statistics according to purse money earned

This would all come later. My siblings and I had to endure what could be described as a volatile childhood. I remember the fighting between my parents and the day my dad packed his bags and moved out. I remember the day my mom moved us to a new town and introduced us to her new *friend*, Randy.

Unfortunately, the friend soon became our step dad and he was not the father-figure he should have been. He was an alcoholic and when he was drunk (which was often) and looking for a fight, he would grab my brother and me by one arm at the top step of the stairs and then kick us in the ass so hard we would fly all the way to the bottom step. I recall how angry and scared I was when the ambulance had to come for my sister after he threw her over the railing and down onto the concrete garage floor, causing her spleen to rupture. We were whipped with horse crops and belts, knocked over our heads with metal spoons, and spanked with the wooden pirate swords my Grandfather had made for my brother and me to play with. Those swords were one inch thick and about two feet long and they left a terrible welt on our back-sides. Grandpa had carefully created them for us at the farm, making sure they didn't have sharp edges or points that could hurt us. They ended up hurting us anyway when we made the mistake of taking them back to Mom's house, where Randy immediately took them away. He stored them on top of the refrigerator and pulled them down anytime he felt one of us needed an *education*.

My mom quickly went through the money she got out of the divorce. She didn't save or invest any of it for the future. She financed Randy's rodeo ambitions, bought him new horses, and paid for new motor homes so we could take off on the weekends to rodeos all over the state. The cops were at our house on countless occasions. Mom would call them when she got scared – and she was scared all the time.

In the end, she finally found the courage to leave Randy. This wasn't easy, because Randy had threatened to kill her and my younger brother, Ben, if she ever tried it. She lost a good 10 years of her life and most of her assets while she was with him. He would later die of a failed liver. My siblings and I lost our identities and our youthful innocence during those years as well as the trust we had always had in our mother to protect us and nurture us. She never recovered financially from the mistakes she made. However, now, at age 70, she is in the midst of a thriving career as a salesperson. She is a fighter and a survivor, which are qualities I know she instilled in me.

My dad is a mink farmer and has been since 1970. Mom petitioned for divorce and left him in 1980 when prices for mink pelts were at all-time highs. This meant he had to pay her more in alimony than would have been required either a year before or a year after. The divorce set him back in many ways, and he never fully recovered from it. My parents both suffered tremendously from their failed marriage, emotionally and financially.

LIFE EVENTS

This is a good opportunity to speak about divorce and how it relates to wealth. Divorce is one of the most devastating events a person can experience. I lived it as a child and then again as an adult – even though I swore that I would never ever get divorced after seeing how it affected me and my siblings. It is hard on families, children and finances. It happens all too often, however, and sometimes it is the only way to move forward with the life you wish to live.

Be smart about your assets during marriage. It is always a good idea to know what is going on with the money. Don't sit back and let your spouse handle it all. Get involved with the family budget.

Have a monthly meeting about savings, expenses, planned purchases and future goals. Track your progress toward those goals. I would recommend hiring a financial advisor to help you both understand your situation and what strategies should be employed to improve your chances of success. I strongly suggest that you keep certain assets such as inheritances or other substantial gifts out of the marital estate. For example, if your parents decide to give you a sizable amount of money, keep those assets in an account titled only in your name. If you commingle those dollars into an account owned jointly with your spouse, they will become part of the marital estate and will be divided up in the event of divorce. Commit to learning as much as you can about investing and financial planning. Divorce doesn't have to crush your financial freedom – and it won't if you are prepared to take charge of your own circumstances.

My dad wasn't really prepared for life on his own. He grew up working on his dad's dairy and crop farm, so farming and ranching was all he ever knew. He wasn't taught how to get ahead by investing and was never comfortable with new technology. He was simply taught to work. He quit school in the 7th grade after losing his right eye in a pitchfork accident. He didn't really enjoy school anyway, and dropping out allowed him to devote more hours to my grandpa and the dairy farm and to spend more time in the fields, planting, harrowing, and harvesting sugar beets, potatoes, and alfalfa for the horses and cattle.

Day after day, year after year, I watched my dad trudge around the farm, feeding, watering and caring for his mink, cows and horses. I was expected to work on the farm, as well. There was no such thing as sleeping in. He would often march into my room in the early morning hours and say, "There's a world out there! Get up and see it for yourself." The grind never really ends on a farm. Animals and crops don't take a day off from needing to be looked after. I gained a lot of my current work ethic and character during those years.

Dad always would have a meeting at the local bank each spring to request enough money in credit to operate the farm for another year until the pelts were sold. The money came in only one time per year and it was nail-biting to wait and see how each year would play out. Would the ranchers make enough to pay off the banker? Or would they need to increase their loans, hoping pelt prices in the coming year would climb back above the cost required to bring them to market?

I didn't like this feeling of borrowing, waiting and hoping. I saw other dads go to work at their normal jobs and have the weekends off with their families. I saw those "regular" dads taking vacations and retiring. Don't get me wrong, I wouldn't trade my dad for the world. He taught me so many valuable lessons in a very quiet way, often by not saying a word. For him and his brothers and all of the other ranchers in our small town, I saw a life of toil and of great uncertainty.

Something about that didn't settle with me. I wanted things to turn out different.

If you're looking for a helpin' hand, try the one
on the other end of your own damn arm.

Cowboy Saying

NO TURNING BACK

I ran away from my mom's house when I was 11. It wasn't the typical runaway story where a kid heads over to his friend's house for a couple of hours. I was angry and I was bullheaded. My mom had taken us away from our dad and forced us to leave our friends, our school, our cousins and grandparents – all of whom lived in our hometown of Morgan. We were allowed to visit our dad every other weekend. Dad had to drive the 34 miles to pick us up every other Friday evening and then drive us back to my mom's on Sunday evening. Those brief days each month with our dad were cherished and so very short.

One morning, Mom and Randy left Ben and me in the back field and gave each of us a shovel. We had orders to chop down the entire half acre of dense four-foot sunflower stocks before they returned home that afternoon. We knew if we didn't get it done in time, we could expect a severe punishment from Randy when he got home. Ben was only 6, and though he tried, he couldn't make much of a dent in a single stock. I chopped and chopped for 20 or 30 minutes, managing to get a couple dozen knocked down but soon realized we were doomed. There was no way we would get this field cleared in a month, let alone one day.

We went in the house to call Dad and ask him for advice on how to cut them down. Not surprisingly, he didn't answer. (There were no cell phones in those days). I called my cousin, who lived next door to my dad and who was only a year older than me. I told him we were unable to do this job and that I wished someone could help us. Hanging up, I felt hot tears come to my eyes. I just wanted us to be back home. I had learned to never show emotion as that was considered weak, so I quickly wiped those tears before Ben noticed and then, in that moment, I made up my mind and there wasn't anything that was going to stop me.

THE JOURNEY

I had a decent 3-speed bike back then, which wasn't too big and wasn't too small. It was light tan with a small, padded seat and had fatter tires than a 10-speed. I had Ben crawl up onto the handle bars and off we went. Looking back, I feel bad for those boys. I especially feel bad for Ben, who never for a second questioned me. He just obeyed and did what I asked him to do. It had to have been the most uncomfortable seven hours of his life.

I knew the way to Morgan from the dozens of trips we had made with Dad back and forth over the past couple of years. We started down our fairly quiet street and made a left onto a slightly busier street, then rode about a mile and turned right onto a very well-traveled main road with a 55 mph speed limit and didn't have more than a couple of feet of shoulder on which to ride. This road would take us into the city of Roy after seven miles of uphill pedaling. Each time the road would get too steep for me to pump both of us up, I would have Ben jump off and run along behind until it flattened out again. Then he would climb back on the handlebars to continue our journey. We made it to Roy after about two hours of riding. I steered into a 7-11 and used the pay phone (luckily I'd brought along some spare change) to call my dad again. No answer. I called my cousin next, as I had his number memorized. I told him we were running away and would hopefully be there by nighttime.

The city of Roy was filled with normal city blocks, stop lights, through streets and double-lane roads on each side. I was a little nervous on the bike but knew what had to be done. We rode for 3 ½ miles and then had to jump off the bike and scamper across the street between passing cars to make the left, which would lead to the freeway entrance. Once we got to the freeway, I exhaled a little bit, because I knew we were out of the congestion. Then the first semi-truck flew by us at 65 mph.

This was a whole new sense of fear. But nothing could stop us at this point. We continued on.

After 10 miles of riding the freeway, we were both getting extremely fatigued. Ben was trying to be tough, but his rear end was getting to the point of bruising and my legs were cramping up. We didn't have any water. Trying to convince both him and myself that we would be okay, I started talking about God and how He would take care of us and that He wanted us to be with Dad.

Ben hung on.

A few miles later, we entered a canyon. The freeway shoulder narrowed and the cars got closer to us. I had to stay totally focused on the lines for fear I would drift over the white and get us both killed. I hoped that a car wouldn't accidentally hit us from behind. Almost as if an angel had been sent to rescue us, we spotted Dad's truck across the river, coming through the canyon in the other direction. Apparently, my cousin, Rich, had notified him of my plans. He exited the west bound side a few miles down and made his way to our side, where he threw my bike in the back of his truck and took us home. We pulled into the farm the most grateful boys in the valley.

Meanwhile, Mom and Randy had returned and found our shovels but not us. Mom was worried and called around looking for us. Finally she called Dad and he confirmed that we were there. Within an hour, she and Randy were pulling in to take us back. We begged and pleaded with Dad, but he believed that his hands were tied. The divorce decree had given Mom full custody and he didn't have any control over what she decided. They hauled us back after we'd spent a grand total of 60 minutes at Dad's after a punishing seven hours getting there.

It wasn't long after that event that Mom decided she was fed up with me and told me to call my dad and go live with him. I was 12 and Ben was 7 at that time. It was both the happiest and saddest day of my life. My dad agreed to come and get me. He was going to the racetrack with my Uncle Tom first, as they had a couple of race horses that needed to be worked out. Knowing they were coming at some point, I packed a small duffle with what I thought I had to have and paced around outside waiting. Mom wouldn't let me take much of anything as she thought I would be begging to come back within a week.

After a few hours, they finally pulled down the road. I didn't even say goodbye to Mom, but Ben had heard the news and got busy packing his little Star Wars duffle bag. He came running around the back of the house and was smiling from ear to ear, ready to go.

Ready to go back home, to stay with me – his brother and trusted ally.

I will never ever forget Dad getting out of the truck, getting down on one knee and holding Ben by each shoulder. He told him that he just couldn't come with us, he was just too young and he needed his Ma for a while longer. Ben slumped his shoulders and looked down, the tears streaming down his cheeks. He was so little and so confused.

What was happening? I cried too, and didn't care if Dad saw me.

"How can we just leave him?" I yelled at Dad, "Why won't you let him come? Why? He needs to come with us, Dad. I won't be here to take care of him!"

Dad got in, closed the door and slowly pulled away while Ben stood on the edge of the street with his little black bag in his hand, watching us go.

"You just broke his heart," I said. I looked at my uncle for help. A tear rolled down his cheek and he looked away. Nobody spoke the rest of the way home.

It was from these experiences that I learned the value of faith. But perhaps more importantly, I learned that if I wanted something, I had better figure out how to make it happen myself.

FIND YOUR PASSION

When I was 13, I started to dream of becoming a professional jockey. My first-ever career dream was to become a professional football player. I held tight to that dream from about age 8 up until age 13, when I realized it was all I could do to tackle guys 50-80 pounds heavier than me and my 105-pound frame.

Mom, to her credit, had always told my siblings and me that we could do whatever we wanted as long as we believed in it enough. I took that advice quite literally with the football aspirations. I didn't have much quit in me and would go up against any of my teammates in line drills. I was the smallest guy on the 13-year-old team by quite a bit, but nonetheless, my coach had me playing both sides – quarterback and inside linebacker. A few times after a really hard hit, I had to pick myself up off the ground with stars flying around in my helmet. Fortunately, I eventually heeded to the advice of my body and locked in on a sport that was more conducive to my size.

I had watched the jockeys galloping Dad's horses and studied how they jacked up their irons so they rode basically standing up, with their hands resting on the horse's neck. I grew particularly excited when it came time to *work* the horses. *Working* a horse means actually letting it run all-out for a certain distance. The horses needed a workout about every three or four weeks to tune them up and get them fit for the actual race, when the money would be on the line. I loved being involved in all aspects of horse racing with my dad, my uncles, and my cousins, from grooming, to saddling and bridling the horses, to legging the jockey up onto the saddle and seeing them work the reins and fit their boots snuggly into the raised stirrups. Each horse took about 10-12 minutes to gallop one mile around the track. The jockey would ride it back, jump off and unsaddle it and then mount another one and do the same thing. The trainers paid the jockeys $5 per gallop and $10 for a workout. I would add up in my mind how much each jockey was making for the afternoon as they hustled around the stable area of the racetrack to exercise horse after horse.

Having been around horses and riding since I was out of casts, it didn't take me long to get the hang of exercising racehorses. I was getting paid $20-$60 a day during the summer galloping and doing full-out breezes of 300 yards. After a few months of this, I was offered an opportunity to ride a horse in my very first race. I accepted, but knew very little about race riding. I relied on what I had observed from watching the others. Leaving the gates on a Quarter Horse is quite a thrill. If you don't know what you're doing, they'll break right out from under you. Zero to 45 in three jumps.

I rode that horse in a five-horse field and won the race. As soon as I had dismounted after the winner's circle photo, another trainer approached me and asked if I would ride his two horses due to race in the third and fourth races.

I asked Dad if it would be okay and he took a good look at the trainer, calculating if this guy knew what he was doing. He always told me to never get on a horse for a trainer who wasn't a good horseman.

"That's how you get hurt," he would say. "Their horses aren't broke to ride and will run right over the rail with you." Apparently, this guy sized up well enough, because Dad said it would be fine for me to ride them, so I rode his horses too, winning one and running second with the other.

A third trainer who had watched me win the earlier races asked if I would ride his Thoroughbred in the last. I'd never even been on a Thoroughbred before, but when he asked how many Thoroughbred races I'd won, I told him that I'd lost count. He apparently liked my answer, because he told me to be ready for the race.

Thoroughbreds have much more stamina than the Quarter Horses I'd been used to riding. They typically run a *minimum* of six furlongs (3/4 of a mile – a furlong is 220 yards) where as a Quarter Horse would typically run 350 yards. A NASCAR versus a dragster. I rode that thoroughbred from start to finish on the lead and won the race. At the end of the day, I pocketed $375 from purse winnings. It was the most money I had ever seen and it was all mine.

WHY DOES ANY OF THIS MATTER?

My racing career started to take wing. I kept collecting gallop money during the week and purse money on the weekends. I felt quite proud of my good fortune. One day, I was sitting with Dad at the local coffee shop as usual for afternoon coffee with the other farmers. They all had their own experiences with horse racing to some extent and would often ask me how things were going.

This day was different, however, and it would profoundly change my life. The older man sitting across from us asked me this question: "Billy, what are you doing with all of that money you're making on the racehorses?" I kind of laughed, and being the bashful kid I was, looked down and said, "I'm saving it."

He pushed deeper. "Where are you saving it at?"

"In my bank account."

At this, he smiled and winked at me. "Let me give you some advice. You need to be investing some of that money, especially at your age. Tomorrow, you come back here and I'll show you what I mean."

Well, I did go back to Jay's diner the next afternoon, and Mr. Tucker opened up the newspaper he had in front of him to the business section, and from there, he pointed to the small print and said, "Right here. This is what you need to do."

The heading said *Mutual Funds* and he scanned down to a bold notation of a fund family. Underneath the heading were about 30 lines of abbreviated fund names with current prices, daily changes and the total return for the year. He told me to use a specific growth fund which invested in U.S.-based large company stocks and explained to me how I would need to go about opening an account. He had taken the liberty of bringing me an account application which had been included with his recent statement. I had never heard of this idea – I could send my money to a company which would invest it in great businesses for me and keep me informed as to the results.

I was only 14 years old at the time I received this investment advice. It would have been very easy to forget or disregard what Mr. Tucker had told me. But thankfully, I'm writing this book because I *didn't* forget it or blow it off. I sent in my application with a check for $250, which was the minimum to get started. Further, I decided to check the box allowing the fund to pull $50 from my checking account each month in order to add to my investment. This was the beginning of something very special.

Wealth is the ability to truly experience life.

HENRY DAVID THOREAU

CHAPTER THREE

COMPOUND RETURNS

Many have called compound interest the eighth wonder of the world. At first, there isn't much to notice. You make a return on your money and feel good about that but you don't get overly enthused. With time, and the right rate of return, seemingly small investments can become colossal.

What is *compound interest*? It's having the interest make interest. When you lump up all of those returns, and then see that addition also provide returns, you start to understand compound returns. Most people understand the term *interest* because they have had some experience with bank accounts and interest is typically a fixed rate which is reported in advance.

Total returns are different. This term refers to the total investment performance for a given period of time. With stocks, the return typically consists of the appreciation of the share price plus the dividend paid. So let's take a hypothetical public company – Ace Fabrication. Assume Ace paid $1.25 per share per year in dividends and the stock appreciated from $20 to $22 during the year. The *total investment return* per share would be $3.25 ($1.25 in dividends and $2 in appreciation). Figuring that as a percentage gain we would take $3.25 and divide that by $20 – which is the investment outlay to purchase one share. In this case the total return would have been 16.25 percent.

Okay – so now we can apply the concepts of compound interest. If we reinvest those dividends into buying more shares, here's what happens:

Let's assume that we had purchased 100 shares of Ace Fab. That outlay was originally $2,000. We received the $1.25 per share over the course of the year (usually divided up and paid equally every quarter). So in total, our dividends produced $125 for the 100 shares. If we had a reinvestment plan in place, we would have purchased approximately six additional shares (This is not exact, as the reinvestment depends on the share price at the time of purchase and we will likely end up with fractional shares.) Now, starting out in year two, we have 106 shares and we get the $1.25 on those shares to give us full-year dividends of $132.50. Repeat the cycle to buy say another seven shares and so now we have 113 shares. Going to year three, we apply the same math and get $141.25. The returns keep piling up. We haven't added a single dime from our own pocket *and* we have some further good news to consider. 1) We will typically expect appreciation of our shares over time as the company grows its earnings. 2) Most companies will increase their dividend payout each year, so the figures will get bumped up with those increases.

Going back to Ace, if we saw a 7 percent average annual share-price appreciation and the company increased its dividend payout by 8 percent annually, here is the projection:

YEAR	SHARE PRICE	ANNUAL DIVIDENDS
1	$20/share	$1.25
2	$21.40	$1.35
3	$22.90	$1.46
4	$24.50	$1.58
5	$26.21	$1.70
6	$28.04	$1.84
7	$30	$1.99
8	$32.10	$2.15
9	$34.35	$2.32
10	$36.75	$2.51

After 10 years, our 100 shares would be worth $3,675 (not including dividends) for a total appreciation of $1,675. This would make the percentage return 84 percent ($1,675/$2,000). Now let's see where the magic comes into play.

The dividends would have paid us $1,815 over that 10 years. If we had reinvested those at an average cost of $27.50, we would have purchased an additional 66 shares along the way, which would make our total share count 166. Multiply that by the ending share price of $36.75 and we arrive at $6,100.50.[11] Our total return, when factoring in the dividends as well, would be 205 percent for the period. The amazing part about this scenario is that we didn't have to do any physical labor and we didn't contribute a cent of additional money from our pocket to the investment. Imagine what would have happened if we had actually kept investing a percentage of our income each month. This is one of my fundamental keys in the steps to becoming wealthy.

------

[11] This is a hypothetical example for illustrative purposes only and does not represent an actual investment. Investor results may vary.

Now keep in mind that some companies don't pay a dividend, and further, share prices can go down during any given period of time. Longer term, stocks provide a more predictable return. Since 1929, U.S. stocks as measured by the S&P 500 have averaged just over 10 percent per year (adjusting for inflation we typically expect a 7 percent real return) but there are many negative years scattered throughout that period of time. The most recent recession in 2008-2009 saw large company stock indexes drop by approximately 45 percent.

Scary times, right? These types of recessions test the nerve of every investor. The key thing to remember when we see a market selloff is that markets have *always* recovered and businesses do everything they can to survive. They become more efficient, and in turn, usually more profitable in the upswing. Being a part-owner in a highly profitable company is a rewarding experience over the long-term.

Here are my Four Rules for Long-Term Investing Success:

1) Start as early as you can.
2) Keep investing regularly using a method called *dollar-cost averaging.*
3) Increase your investment contributions commensurate with your income (at least ten percent of income, but 15 percent is my recommendation).
4) Don't panic when market declines occur. Actually, do the opposite and get excited. This is your opportunity to buy more shares while prices are on sale.

"I will tell you the secret to getting rich on Wall Street.
You try to be greedy when others are fearful.
And you try to be fearful when others are greedy."

WARREN BUFFETT

RULE OF 72

For those who enjoy forecasting and using variables, the rule of 72 is a fun investing concept that can solve for various outcomes. It's a mathematical formula whereby you divide 72 by the rate of return to obtain the number of years it will take for an investment to double. So, for example, assume a 10 percent total return. Divide 72 by 10 and you get 7.2. This means that if you invest your money and average a 10 percent annual return, your money will double in 7.2 years.

I use the following exercise in the financial boot camp and it may be the thing students most remember. I started teaching the power of doubling periods in 1998 when I was asked to speak at a youth leadership conference. The basic skill I was trying to teach to this room full of young teenagers was that starting an investment program early in life is super important in order to create long-term wealth. I used a common scenario so they could all feel the real possibility they could see results. I suggested to them that they find a way to earn $2,000. Earning that sum of money was a bit harder back in 1998 than it is today but was still very possible. Students shouted out ideas. They could mow lawns, deliver newspapers, tend children, do odd jobs, etc. Even if they received some help from Mom and Dad or Grandpa and Grandma, this amount of money would be the seeds for their investment portfolios and for the orchard that could grow from it.

I used a starting age of 14 because this was the average age of the attendees, and also the approximate age at which I started investing. Stock market (equity) returns will vary and regulators require advisors like me to attach all sorts of disclaimers about historical facts. Projecting future returns is even more restrictive. Having said that, we try to base our future returns on data markets have provided over many decades. While showing 8 percent would be considered more proper by state and federal regulators, to simplify calculations in this illustration I'll show a total return of 10 percent, which is used by many in the industry as a historical average annual rate of return for stocks. Therefore, the initial investment of $2,000 would double to $4,000 in 7.2 years. For simplification, I used a seven-year doubling period rather than 7.2. Seven is easy to compound for you football fans.

AGE	INVESTMENT VALUE
14	$2,000.00
21	$4,000.00
28	$8,000.00
35	$16,000.00
42	$32,000.00
49	$64,000.00
56	$128,000.00
63	$256,000.00
70	$512,000.00
77	$1,024,000.00

After I draw out these doubling periods on the whiteboard on which $2,000 turns into $1,024,000, I return to the earlier question posed to the financial literacy boot camp attendees. "Who among you will be a millionaire someday?" More hands go up this time, though not all. Some people just don't have the initiative to make that first move. Growing up on a farm gave me a lot of old punch lines and comebacks. In this case we would say, "*You can lead the horses to water, but you can't make 'em drink.*"

To take this example out a little further, let's actually assume the person (notice I haven't referred to him as an investor yet) became motivated after seeing the first doubling period, so at age 21 he decided to start a dollar-cost averaging program of $200 per month. He continues this monthly investment until reaching age 61 and then he stops. This is very reasonable, as this would mean investing 10 percent of a $24,000 per year income. Here is how that scenario might play out: With the same 10 percent return, the total value would be $1,490,158 at age 61.

Missing just one doubling period can have a dramatic effect. Assume now that the person waits until age 21 rather than age 14 to invest his initial $2,000, and then begins the $200 per month contribution at age 28 rather than age 21. In this scenario, the investor will end up with a value of $729,992.[12]

When we assist retirees with their lifetime income stream from their retirement portfolios, we generally recommend a 4.5 percent withdrawal rate for the first dozen years or so, and then possibly increase the withdrawal rate if the plan is on track and no extra distributions have impacted the principal. If we considered a 4.5 percent withdrawal on the two different ending values above, we would be looking at an annual spending amount of $67,056 versus an amount of $32,849. Still a large sum of money, but there is the possibility of a much different lifestyle for the person who chose to act at age 14.

For those who did wait and are now wondering if they should just toss this book or go walk out into traffic, don't despair. You still have hope to rectify your situation. It will just take some extra work. Playing catch-up is quite common in the financial arena and one reason Congress enacted a law allowing investors over age 50 to contribute more to IRAs, Roth IRAs and other types of retirement plans than those under 50. They aptly named this law the *catch-up provision*.

---

[12] This is a hypothetical example for illustrative purposes only and does not represent an actual investment. Investor results may vary.

Ramp up your investment contributions as high as possible. Cut back on discretionary spending and get your debt under control. Work to pay off any high-interest debt first and then continue to attack other debts until all that is left is good debt, such as a mortgage or interest on an asset that will appreciate rather than depreciate.

If you've missed out on some of the time value, you now need to sacrifice non-essential spending in favor of investing. This is necessary unless you are one of the fortunate folks staring at a large inheritance, marrying into money, hitting the lottery, starting a successful business and selling it or patenting an amazing product. Investing in the market is a passive activity – at least, it is with the advice I'm giving. I do not advocate day trading, timing the market or attempting to profit from speculation in penny stocks. Those strategies are extremely hard to make money in and a vast number of people have lost fortunes falling into those traps.

Bottom line, time is your friend when it comes to investing. You only have so much of it, so don't waste a single day to get started, even if it's small at first.

The secret of getting ahead is getting started.

MARK TWAIN

KEEP YOUR WITS

There have been dozens of well-documented investment manias throughout history. Each one ended about the same – with empty pockets and lost dreams. Why do we keep making the same mistakes?

The definition of insanity is doing the same thing over and over and expecting a different outcome. Humans can be very predictable creatures. The Wall Street axiom *"Buy Low – Sell High"* is well known and seemingly understood by investors, yet a small fraction of them follow that advice. For the majority, when they see others gaining, they want to gain. When they see prices dropping, they want their money back. Early on in an investment bubble when the prices are reasonable, interest in the particular asset rises and valuations move higher. As the news spreads and more people take notice of the riches being created, speculation takes hold. This is where creative people attempt to profit on a larger scale by multiplying their positions and borrowing to do so. In the financial industry we often hear this quote from Mark Twain – *"History doesn't repeat itself, but it quite often rhymes."* If you haven't noticed, I like Mark Twain. He was a straight-shooter and had a dry wit I personally find very enjoyable. To drive the point home about speculation and that I do expect another craze to take place in this country during the 21st century, I will share with you some examples of investing manias.

In the early 1600's, the Dutch people living in the Netherlands had become fascinated with tulips. The flower had become a certain religious symbol and also was thought to be a sign of wealth and good fortune. The affluent merchants started buying tulip bulbs for their wives and mistresses. Soon, a market developed whereby traders would sell interests in future bulbs that weren't even sprouted yet (speculation), and the craze spread like wild fire. Single bulbs were being sold for what a high-end home in Holland would cost. Many people invested their life fortunes in future bulb crops, betting on the likelihood that someone else would buy their bulbs for much more in the coming months. Then, after everyone was comfortable and giddily riding the wave of higher and higher prices, the bubble burst.

It started when a tulip bulb auction in Amsterdam was unattended, leading to news that these sellers were unable to unload their bulbs. This prompted bulb owners to bring their holdings to different auctions in hopes of selling before prices declined. The oversupply of sellers combined with an undersupply of buyers forced the prices to spiral downward. The once-held belief that prices of bulbs were stable and dependable quickly vanished. Valuations plummeted and never went back to the peak levels again.

Since humans tend to repeat the same mistakes, we would expect something like this to happen again. In 1711, the year that the South Sea Company was created, it did. The main purpose for its formation was to exchange **debt** owed by Great Britain to investors, into **stock** in a company that would potentially reward the investors with a much-greater return. The excitement in the company stock was based on the theory that the South Sea Company would control trade in Central and South America. Shares in the company skyrocketed from 100 British pounds in early 1719 to more than 1,000 pounds in 1720, a 1,000 percent return in just over a year. For perspective, a British pound in 1750 (the earliest date for which I could get data) would be worth about 220 pounds today. Thus 1,000 pounds in 1720 had the purchasing power of 220,000 pounds in 2019 (279,302 U.S. dollars). One share of stock was worth more than a ship, most homes and a lifetime of wages. The underlying, but unknown problem was that the company didn't actually have any dominant position with any trading partners. To keep the scheme going, the founders began selling shares at a 30 percent upfront discount to new investors and even offered people loans to buy more shares. When a handful of investors asked to redeem their shares, the company couldn't produce the capital to buy the shares back. This news spread and led to the crumbling of the share price. And the rest is history.

More recent examples of investment bubbles were the Dot-com Bubble of the mid 1990's, the real-estate frenzy in the early 2000's, the oil price spike, which saw the price of a barrel of oil rise from less than $25 in 2003 to a peak of $147.30 in 2008, and the Bitcoin Bubble in 2017. Back in 2016, a single bitcoin could be purchased for less than $500. By May of 2017, the price had surged to $2,000. New-age tech nerds came out of the woodwork and began proclaiming that this new crypto currency was going to change the world of payments, effectively replacing the dollar. By December of 2017, the price had jumped an astonishing amount to *$19,783* per bitcoin. Crypto investors defended the price and taunted those who *just didn't get it*. Their online posts were bold and brash, predicting that bitcoin was part of a new block chain paradigm and the mathematics of this paradigm made it impossible for bitcoin to decline in price. Predictably, bitcoin soon began its descent and dropped all the way down to $3,183 by December 15, 2018. A few short months later, there appears to be a second wave of bitcoin speculation taking place, as the price surged back to more than $11,865 per coin on June 28, 2019. Then, in one single trading day on July 1, 2019, the price plummeted by over $2,000. That is a 17 percent drop in value in less than eight hours. This wild ride of volatility has all happened in a very short window of time relative to most investments. I personally believe it is pure speculation and not a solid investment for the long term.

During the Internet Bubble, companies that had anything to do with online information, sales, or those that made the networking equipment which allowed businesses and individuals to connect digitally, started forming and attempting to take themselves public. IPOs (Initial Public Offerings) were all the rage. Almost all investors wanted to get shares on the IPO, and it didn't really matter what the company's business model was. I was a fledgling advisor in the late

1990's and saw this up close. When a company made its announcement to go public, brokerage houses scrambled to get involved in the underwriting syndicate. If they were selected to the selling group, they would begin the process of determining how many shares to make available to each of their most valued clients. Often, a client would purchase the shares on the offering date and then sell them as soon as the restriction was lifted – generally three days.

Back then, it was extremely likely that shares would trade higher from the opening market price. Priceline.com went public in March of 1999 at $18 per share and ended the day trading north of $82 per share. eBay went public on September 21, 1998 at $18 per share and ended the day more than $53 per share. Amazon shares opened at $18 and reached $100 per share before the Dot-com Bubble burst in a little more than two years (a 455 percent return). The NASDAQ, which is the exchange most utilized for technology stock trading, rose from a level of 1,000 in 1995 to over 5,000 in the year 2000. That's a 400 percent return in just five years. The difference between *perceived* value and *actual* value created the bubble. People wanted in. They heard about neighbors, friends, brothers-in-law or colleagues who were making tens of thousands on Internet stocks and greed took its normal spot at the table. It always shows up when a feast is piled high.

The dam broke in 2000 and most technology stocks began a steady decline. By October 2002, the NASDAQ had lost 78 percent of its value. Many unprofitable companies went completely bankrupt. Shareholders typically lose everything when a company declares bankruptcy. Pets.com took itself public in February 2000 at $11 per share. The shareholders saw their stock prices fall to 19 cents by November 2000 and the company filed for bankruptcy. eToys had similar results, although it gave shareholders some false excitement along the way. Going public at $20 per share in May of 1999, it ended

68

its first day as a public company trading at $76 per share. Within two years, however, the stock had fallen to just nine cents, and those shareholders who'd speculated on the company's future were left with a bag of bones. Some companies survived because they had better financial strength, but they certainly saw their share prices decline. Amazon, for example, had raised approximately $600 million in a bond offering just a few weeks prior to the descent, and that move allowed it to survive the storm.

Even if you're on the
right track, you'll get run
over if you just sit there.

WILL ROGERS

CHAPTER FOUR

BROADEN
YOUR HORIZONS

A typical day for me when I was in the height of my riding career was to ride seven or eight different horses on the racing card. Having more races to ride gave me a better chance of coming home with at least one winner for the day. My agents (I had two different agents during my career) knew this concept well and would hustle from trainer to trainer, attempting to lock up mounts on different horses for different races. If they had only been concerned with securing mounts for one specific type of horse or race, I would have likely ended up with far fewer mounts, and in turn, fewer victories. For me, this ability to diversify across race types meant being able to ride a Quarter Horse in a 350-yard race, followed perhaps by a one-mile Thoroughbred contest in the very next race. Most other jockeys specialized in one breed or the other. You wouldn't see Eddie Delahoussaye riding a Quarter Horse, nor would you see Jerry Nicodemus on a Thoroughbred. The shotgun approach worked best for me as I wanted to ride as many races as possible — spreading out the opportunities to win, and also the risks of losing.

Diversification is a risk-management strategy that mixes a wide variety of investments within a portfolio, according to Investopedia. The rationale behind this technique is that a portfolio constructed of different kinds of assets will, on average, yield smoother long-term returns and lower the risk of any individual holding or security. Slow and steady wins *this* race. Having a larger basket of eggs is more attractive than a smaller basket with only a couple of eggs. But further than that, why not have multiple baskets? Each basket may have different kinds of assets such as stocks, bonds, cash, real estate, collectibles, etc.

Sometimes we look at diversification as a drag on the better-performing assets. After all, to be truly diversified means you will always have underperforming investments as part of the overall pie. When you're invested in the winning team, diversification can feel like a dumb idea. Why bet on a horse that has recently shown a losing race record? It's hard to keep money in a lagging, or worse, a declining investment when your other investments are doing so much better. But it's important to remember today's top performer quite often becomes a laggard at some point. Here is a chart detailing the annual returns for various asset classes over a 20-year period.

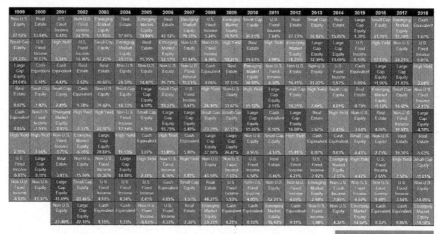

The Callan Periodic Table of Investment Returns

Annual Returns for Key Indices Ranked in Order of Performance (1999–2018)

The Callan Periodic Table of Investment Returns conveys the strong *case for diversification* across asset classes (stocks vs. bonds), capitalizations (large vs. small), and equity markets (U.S. vs. non-U.S.). The Table highlights the uncertainty inherent in all capital markets. Rankings change every year. Also noteworthy is the difference between absolute and relative performance, as returns for the top-performing asset class span a wide range over the past 20 years.

20th Anniversary Edition

Callan | Knowledge. Experience. Integrity.

© 2019 Callan LLC

Cycles are normal and to be expected. Investment sectors and asset classes have their rotations. It's quite difficult to predict which will be the top performer or the bottom performer in any given year, let alone any month or week. Notice the shadings don't hold any specific pattern. The best-performing asset category in one year may change and become a middle-of-the-road or low-end performer just a year later. Basing future investment strategies solely off of what worked last year is often the wrong move. I call this rear-view mirror investing. To go forward, you must look at the road ahead of you.

STAND YOUR GROUND

Avoiding big overall losses is a key factor here, but we as a species are very susceptible to emotions – the main ones being fear and greed. For example, investors who got sucked into the technology craze back in the late 1990's during what is now known as the Dot-com Bubble may have felt pretty good for a while with a basket of technology stocks. The returns for tech stocks back in those days was borderline hysteria. People weren't concerned if earnings were being reported, much less if they were in the black. The main driver of stock prices was the *expectation* for positive earnings sometime in the future. Why get too concerned about a trivial thing such as profits when the Internet had changed the world. Right? This time it would be different. Right?

Wrong. *Greed* had pushed prices to unsustainable levels. When the value of anything rises that high that quickly, a painful correction is typically necessary to wash out the excess. Most times, the washing out pushes prices down much further than necessary. The pendulum swings back well past center. This is due to the other emotion – *fear*. People sell their holdings in a frenzy just at the time when valuations are likely at their best. My advice for young investors, and even aged investors, is to avoid the crowd at extremes. I'm not sure who first penned that term, but it is very useful when it comes to investing. No matter what the situation, crowds have a tendency to show up at times when things are wonderful and also when they are terrible.

In the former, the crowd has come together in a money grab. In the latter, the crowd has gathered in a panic. Sometimes investors base their investment decisions on headlines or whatever is happening in the world. One can easily find a reason *not* to invest at any given time period. In the 1940's, Pearl Harbor was bombed and the Cold War began. In the 1950's, events such as the Korean War, Soviets detonating an H-bomb and a late recession caused worry. The Berlin Wall was erected in the 1960's, followed by the Cuban Missile Crisis and Kennedy's assassination. The 1970's brought Watergate, an oil embargo, Nixon's resignation and an energy crisis. Reagan and the Pope were both shot in the 1980's, followed by the worst recession in more than 40 years and the junk bond market collapse. In the 1990's, Iraq invaded Kuwait, we saw riots in Los Angeles and the Federal Reserve raised interest rates six times. In the first decade of the 21st Century, we had the worst terrorist attack in U.S. history, with both of the World Trade Center towers crumbling to the ground. Further, the U.S. entered the Gulf War with Iraq, numerous corporate accounting scandals erupted and we saw the bursting of the Internet Bubble. Most recently, we have experienced a severe recession caused by the housing collapse, which sent the unemployment rate to more than 10 percent, the European debt crisis, Brexit, and extreme political uncertainty. Through all of these terrible events, markets survived, businesses moved forward and investors did well by staying the course. A great number of mutual funds have provided investors with impressive returns over decades. I have a lot of personal experience with several funds both for my own money as well as my clients'.

The earliest mutual fund in America was incepted in 1924 and opened to investors in 1928. It has provided an average annual return of approximately 8 percent per year through June 2019. Another well-known fund came into existence in 1934 with a bit better timing, since it avoided the Great Depression. The average annual return for that stock fund has been 12.4 percent per year through June 2019. If a person had invested in that fund during various periods of uncertainty – trusting in capitalism and the professional fund managers at the helm, he would have been well rewarded. For example, a $10,000 investment in this fund on the day of the invasion of Pearl Harbor would be worth $69,062,104 at the end of 2018. Investing $10,000 on the day John F. Kennedy was assassinated would have grown to $3,821,738 by year end, 2018. Even more recently when markets became fragile with the terrorist attacks in New York, investing $10,000 on the day of the attack would have grown to $35,088 by 2018. Understandably, one doesn't often think about capitalizing in the face of such devastating events. People died and our focus was not, nor should it have been on individual gains.

These examples are illustrated simply to show that our country has survived serious tragedies. Each of these events caused significant market sell-offs in the days and weeks afterward. In every case, the markets recovered and climbed to new highs. We are resilient through the toughest of times, so the next event that drives the media frantic with headlines such as political turmoil or interest rate policies, remember to keep all of this in perspective. Forcing yourself to invest during negative events is hard. Uncertainty is a very uncomfortable emotion and it causes people to freeze up, to wait and see, to become complacent. That is why we advocate the automatic investment approach called *dollar-cost averaging*. This allows your contributions or purchases to happen routinely – without any thought or action on your part.

Investing and dieting are somewhat the same. Most people would love to adopt a plan for both and actually stick with them. They have great intentions at the on-set but things go wrong in the follow through.

I have considerable experience with both and I'm here to tell you, investing is so much easier. During my riding career, I was required to maintain a weight of 112 pounds. Keeping my 5'6" body at that weight was very difficult. I was a complete anorexic. I actually got a thrill out of lowering my weight. I took great pains to avoid food. My daily intake consisted of coffee, a few pretzels, a small salad and a 3 Musketeer's® bar to give me enough energy to ride a full day of races. Jockeys are required to stand on the scales up to 20 times per day. They are weighed one hour before the first race of the day in order to determine if they will be over or under their assigned weights for each horse, and then again immediately before and after each race they ride to ensure that no cheating was involved. When people would say, "Oh, you're like a wrestler then," I would laugh. Wrestlers weigh-in one time — 30 minutes or so prior to their assigned matches. Once weighed, they are free to re-hydrate and re-nourish their bodies. No-can-do for jockeys. The riding weight must be maintained throughout the day. I would often see stars attempting to pull up my mount after a race, due to the fact I was so weak. Most riders are bulimic, forcing themselves to purge (flip) every bite of food they eat in order to maintain the weight that allows them to continue getting mounts. Each racetrack has a *Jocks Room* which is like a locker room/spa/entertainment room all in one. The main fixtures in each Jocks Room are scales, televisions, pool tables, a sauna (hot box), a steam room, and a flipping bowl. A flipping bowl is a modified toilet that doesn't have a seat and is extra wide to allow for puking. Dieting is taken to a whole new level.

The point I'm making is, investing doesn't have to feel like dropping weight every day. You can turn on the automatic feature to handle the contributions and then simply monitor your progress, making changes if necessary. If possible, do what you can to increase those investment amounts when it feels the hardest. If history is any proof, you'll be glad you did. On the other hand, when investing seems easy and the risk feels very low, it may be time to rein back your horses a little. These periods can also prove difficult to navigate because the prices just keep going up. The news media can't stop talking about the money being made. Grandma and Grandpa have decided to jump in and everyone is just down-right happy. Stretches like these are actually more risky than when markets sell off.

During my career as a financial advisor, I have seen many market cycles, large upswings and many equally large downswings. Sentiment can change quickly, largely due to the fact that securities such as publicly traded stocks are so widely followed each and every day. Shares can be bought and sold in a matter of seconds. This fact alone has led to the creation of countless computerized trading systems seeking to profit from fractions of a penny movements in stock prices. These systems use algorithms in an attempt to predict the slightest of price changes. When a trend is ascertained, the system may buy a very large position of an individual security or stock index in one second and sell the entire position a few seconds later. The result of this high volume in trading is volatility. Too much volatility perpetuates high levels of anxiety for individual investors, thus sparking many of them to begin selling, which creates even more volatility. The initial selling breeds more selling, causing the spiral to become a state of fear-based selling, having nothing much to do with economic outlook or corporate profits.

———————————— 66 ————————————

Investing should be more like watching paint dry or watching grass grow. If you want excitement, take $800 and go to Las Vegas.

PAUL SAMUELSON

The best investing advice I ever received was this: *"Do the opposite of what your emotions want you to do."* It's very hard to invest at the time your fear is high. It's much easier to make that same investment when everything is positive and markets are rising. The main difference is that when markets are negative, prices are cheaper. I still remember a quote from a very successful investor by the name of Shelby Cullom Davis, which I first heard in 1998. *"You make most of your money in a bear market; you just don't realize it at the time."* (A Bear Market is one that is declining. A Bull Market is one that is advancing.) This means you should not fear a down market while you are in your accumulation years. You should actually welcome it. Mr. Davis has some clout in the financial world as he parlayed an initial investment of $100,000 in the 1940's into more than $800 million by the time he retired in the early 1990's. Another favorite saying of mine during a period of market turmoil is *"Hurry up and don't do something."* Let the sellers sell, be patient, and then do exactly the opposite. Buying during market declines can be extremely beneficial to your wealth. Buying high can make wealth creation take longer. Speculating can completely destroy it.

Let's address how listening to the wrong people can potentially keep you from having any success with your financial future. Let's examine the story of John and Walt:

John and Walt sat in their usual spots in the local café drinking coffee the same way they had done for 30 years. People came and went, hurrying in for morning breakfasts and then hurrying back out with places to go and things to do. John and Walt never paid much attention to the outsiders. They spent most mornings discussing important issues, such as the weather, local community events, the obituaries and of course, politics. Today, however, they ended up having a conversation unlike any other.

At around 9:15 a.m., just as they were finishing their first cup, an elderly gentleman of about 80 years old walked in, who appeared to be in no big hurry, unlike the usual patrons. He had a smile on his face and a surprising bounce in his step for a man his age. With a newspaper folded under one arm, he asked if he might sit down with the men.

John said, "Sure, have a seat. We were just discussing this crazy country, Obama and the stock market. Ha ha. Walt here came into some money recently and decided it would be smart to invest in the stock market. I tried to tell him it was a crazy idea. Heck, it's plain to see the stock market is rigged."

The waitress approached and refilled both coffee cups then asked if she could bring anything to the newcomer. The old man ordered two scrambled eggs, wheat toast and a Coca-Cola.

When she walked away, John continued. "I'm John and this here's Walt, as I mentioned."

The old man shook both of their hands and said, "Nice to meet you. I'm traveling through and saw this little café, so I thought I would stop in for a bite. I enjoy getting to visit with locals in every town I travel through."

Both Walt and John chuckled. "Well, I can tell you we've seen it all in this town," said Walt. "Whatever you want to know, just ask."

After some time had passed discussing local town issues about which John and Walt both expressed their anti-growth views, the old man asked John to elaborate on his feelings about investing.

"So, John, why do you feel the stock market is rigged?"

Without missing a beat, John said, "I've followed that thing for years now and I watch the nightly news. The market is up, the market is down – it's a fool's game, and I know lots of folks who've lost everything in that darned thing. You can't trust those slick Wall Street boys. They'll skin you like a cat. I wouldn't put a dime into that market and I've told Walt a dozen times that he doesn't have a chance in hell. Have you seen how high that thing is? Last time it got up to this level, it crashed and burned and people lost their whole life savings. Doesn't take a genius to see what's coming. I'm keeping my money in the bank where it's safe and sound."

The man nodded and took another sip of his Coke, allowing those words to hang in the air a moment. Then, turning to Walt, he asked, "Do you feel *good* or *bad* about your investment decision, Walt?"

Stammering a bit, Walt said, "Well I guess I'm not quite sure yet. My son has been investing in it for a long time and he claims he has done really well."

"Heh," said John. "I'll bet he's lost his you-know-what just like everybody else, if he were being totally honest."

Partially acknowledging that possibility, Walt continued on. "I don't claim to be an expert or anything like that. I see it go up one month and back down the next. I see that most of the time the markets are reacting to one thing or another and it's kinda frustrating, to be honest. Why should a newspaper report in China about a slowdown in Chinese construction wreak havoc on the entire United States market? I'm wondering if John may be right. What do you think yourself, sir? Say, we didn't catch your name."

The old man wiped his mouth and said, "I understand your concern and your frustration. If you watch the news or read the papers, you'll see a hundred opinions on what to do with your investments, and they can change from minute to minute. I have a fair amount of experience in this area, so let me tell you what I know. I've been investing for nearly all of my adult life – close to 65 years now. In my experience and opinion, I have found the markets to be very rewarding. First of all, you aren't exactly investing in the *stock market* per se. You're simply using the market as a means to purchase shares in a company or companies you wish to own. Take those cups of coffee there you are both drinking. My guess is the coffee is made by Folgers, of which I'm sure you're familiar. JM Smucker Company owns Folgers and a whole host of other well-known brands such as Jif, Carnation, Eagle Brand, Sara Lee, Pillsbury, Hungry Jack, Crisco and many others to go along with their famous Smucker's jellies and jams. JM Smucker Company has been in existence since 1897 and they have a very long history of providing shareholders with meaningful returns. So instead of looking at the investment landscape as a sea of confusion with rapid buying and selling, Wall Street scandals and risk, I would offer a different view. Consider it a mechanism, which allows small-timers like you and me the opportunity to invest in great companies with great management teams and share in the extraordinary system we know as capitalism. For most of its existence, JM Smucker has been a private company, but on June 28, 2002, the private owners decided to take the company public. That means they listed the company on the New York Stock Exchange under the symbol SJM, and offered it for sale to the general investing public. Now, if you could go back and invest in that company on its public offering, would you?"

Walt and John looked at each other and then said in unison, "I would."

"Wise decision, gentlemen," said the man. "If you had each invested just $10,000 in the company stock on that day, you would both be sitting on over $38,000 in SJM stock and would have received several more thousand in dividends along the way. You would have seen the shares fluctuate wildly over those years, but through it all, you would have continued to receive your dividends and see your investment compound at close to 20 percent per year growth over that 14-year period."

The old man went on about this company and that, still without offering his name, but by now, John and Walt didn't care, as they were too busy contemplating his explanation of how downright simple things really were when you stepped back and looked at how companies made profits and how shareholders *shared* in those profits.

"I heard you say that you watch the nightly news, John."

"Yep. Every night. And I see that Dow Jones jumping all over the place. I just don't trust the market. It seems like the big boys have the system rigged so they make all the money."

"Well, I can see how someone might feel that way, especially if he watches the market daily and expects it to go up and never down," the man said. "I also hear the commentators sparking fear into the minds of small investors whenever markets decline. It's no wonder the average investor feels he has no chance in a market now dominated by erratic investing habits of the hedge funds and day traders who think they have figured out the price movements before they happen. But this conclusion is dead wrong — such markets are ideal for any investor, small or large, so long as he sticks to his guns. When shareholders react to news and decide to toss their shares back into the pool in mass quantities, share prices may fall. The extent of the decline is directly related to the amount of hysteria amongst the owners. If they fear the worst and suddenly assume that a solid company like JM Smucker is no longer going to be in business, or that the share price will plummet to zero, shares will, in many cases, be available for purchase at lower prices.

"This type of opportunity is why I love the stock market. It allows me to purchase stock in great companies at what I consider to be inexpensive prices from so-called *investors* who want nothing more than to discard their shares and convert them back into cash. Every single market decline, correction, crash, bear market or otherwise period of lower stock prices has been followed by a new high for the overall stock market. The S&P 500 has averaged slightly over 10 percent since 1926.[13] That would have been realized only if an investor was truly disinterested in the various downturns, which is why most people never invest in stocks. They can't handle the uncertainty, so they sacrifice what could be have been a very prosperous endeavor. So no, the stock market isn't rigged. It just sometimes feels that way with all of the in-and-out trading going on. Remember, every *sale* requires an opposite and equal *buy* in order to make a transaction happen. Someone or some institution will end up owning those shares. I propose that you decide to be an investor and long-term owner and not forsake your interest in a good company or companies just because the share prices temporarily went down."

The old man sat back and finished off his Coke. Looking at his empty glass, he said, "I've owned Coca-Cola stock for over 50 years. I can tell you with certainty that I have benefitted handsomely over those years and love the idea that people all over the globe are purchasing Coca-Cola products every minute of every day. I'm sharing in those profits. As a matter of fact, do you know how much a $40 investment in one share of Coca-Cola stock would be worth today if you had purchased it in 1919 when Coke went public?"

"I'd guess a fair amount," said John. "Say around thirty grand?"

Walt shrugged and said, "I'm more optimistic than John, so I'll guess it would be worth fifty thousand."

---

[13] "Vanguard Portfolio Allocation Models." *Portfolio Allocation Models,* https://personal.vanguard.com/us/insights/saving-investing/model-portfolio-allocations.

Their new friend chuckled and cleared his throat. "The actual value would be nearly $400,000 if you had taken all dividends in cash. And if you had reinvested all of the dividends, your $40 investment would be worth $9.8 million today."

Walt choked on his coffee and wiped his mouth.

John stared in disbelief. "Is that really possible?"

"It's as sure as the sun setting," said the man.

With that, the old man placed $7 on the table to cover his breakfast, picked up his paper and rose to leave. "I wish you both the best of luck. Walt, I would build up your investment account with the help of an advisor who understands the concepts I've laid out here today. It's the *time* owning stocks, not the *timing* of owning them that matters. Don't become emotional when prices decline and decide to sell out, as so many people do."

Turning to John, he said, "Nobody loses everything by buying high quality, profitable companies and holding those shares for a long stretch of time or forever – which is my favorite holding period. What *actually* happens is people sell their holdings at the market low and accept a loss in value – sometimes a steep loss. Or sometimes, the investments made were not well thought out and could be better classified as speculation rather than investing. Unproven businesses will often fail. I do not advise chasing hype or highly-leveraged and unprofitable businesses."

Both Walt and John stood and extended their hands. "Thanks a million," said John. "I think I need to re-evaluate my plans."

Walt felt a huge relief wash over him as he shook the old man's hand. "I'm sure glad you happened by this morning. You make a lot of sense. Where are you from?"

"I come from Omaha. Lived there my whole life. My friends call me Warren. It was nice meeting you both." With that, the oracle of Omaha smiled and walked out the door.

I wrote this story a few years ago to provide a bit of perspective into what type of coffee shop banter I heard growing up in a small town. It seemed logical that people would frame their opinions of investment professionals and even investment strategies by what they heard from friends and neighbors. Fortunately for me, I had my first encounter with investing from Mr. Tucker, who was a big proponent of investing, and this positively shaped my opinion of such matters. I later realized that people are afraid of what they don't know.

With investing, these fears are most often unfounded. Just because your parents or family members have never invested or have nothing good to say about it doesn't make it bad. To be sure, Wall Street has had its share of controversy and scandals. In my 23-year career, I have seen dozens of corporate executives come under fire for accounting fraud, insider trading and other securities-based crimes. The images of Wall Street stock brokers and investment bankers and even hedge fund managers have taken a serious blow in the last few years as a result of these highly-publicized crimes. Perceptions were further weakened by the severe housing recession which currently still looms in the minds of those who lived through it.

On the other hand, the media does a great job of taking things too far. Get comfortable with headlines that seem to require your attention or demand some type of action on your part. I would suggest that 95 percent of these *urgent* news stories are irrelevant to your investment strategy. Don't get caught up in the day-to-day events. Find time to do things you enjoy and give your mind a break from the worries, stress and anxiety we all seem to create for ourselves.

I've had a lot of worries in my life,
most of which never happened.

MARK TWAIN

THE WINNER'S CIRCLE

Today, Amazon is a global powerhouse and the largest company in the world, based on market capitalization. (This is calculated by multiplying the number of shares outstanding by the per-share price.) If you had been fortunate and purchased just $2,000 of Amazon stock on the IPO you would be quite wealthy today. For fun, here's the calculation: $2,000/$18 (the IPO price) = 111 shares. Amazon has split three times since its IPO. Once at two-for-one in 1998, which doubled your share count to 222. Another two-for-one occurred in early 1999, doubling your shares again to 444, and again in late 1999 – this time three-for-one, which left you with 1,332 shares. Today Amazon trades at $2,008/share[14] so your original $2,000 investment would now be worth **$2,674,656!** Are you impressed? I certainly hope so.

But let's be honest. Most people weren't able to purchase shares at the IPO price and had to wait until the shares became publicly available on the stock exchange. In that case, the share price may have been higher, and therefore your $2,000 purchased fewer shares. Assume you waited a few days and purchased your shares at $25 per share. Your $2,000 would have bought 80 shares. Today, you would own 960 shares with a value of $1,663,680. This is very much still a wonderful investment. The return for Amazon shareholders has been extraordinary. To be fair, most companies provide more modest growth rates, yet still offer shareholders a solid return on investment over time.

Take Apple, for example. It wasn't thought of as a must-own company until many years after it launched the Macintosh computer. Apple's real potential with mainstream consumers began with the

---

[14] Price as of July 15, 2019

launch of the iPod. It has become a true American success story, which has made countless shareholders very wealthy.

Apple went public in December of 1980 at a price of $22 per share. The company has split its stock on four different occasions. In 1987, they split two-for-one. In 2000, they split two-for-one. In 2005, they split two-for-one and in 2014 they split seven-for-one. So, if you purchased $2,000 of Apple stock at the $22 offering price, you would have owned 90.9 shares. To keep the math simple, we'll assume you just bought 90 shares. (You would likely have paid a hundred or so dollars in commission anyway.) Progressively, your 90 shares became 180 shares after the split in 1987. The 180 shares became 360 shares in 2000. Those 360 shares became 720 shares in 2005. Then the big split of seven times turned your share count into 5,040 in 2014. Today, Apple trades at a price of approximately $202 per share.[15] Your total investment grew from $2,000 to **$1,018,080**, a 50,804 percent return. Apple has traded at an all-time high of $233.47 per share, which would have valued your shares at **$1,176,688**.

Now on the surface, stock splits appear to instantly give shareholders more value, but that's not really the case. When a company splits its stock, the share price is adjusted on the same basis as the split. In a two-for-one split, your shares double and the stock price halves. In a four-for-one split, your shares quadruple and the share price is reduced to a quarter of what it was. The total value is still equal after a split, so why do companies even do it? The biggest reason corporate boards do this is to provide the ability for the average investor to purchase stock. Most people like to buy shares in round lots rather than purchase a certain dollar amount. A round lot is 100 shares. Therefore, if a company's share price climbs to $500 per share,

---

[15] Price as of July 11, 2019

it would require $50,000 to purchase a round lot of 100 shares, and most investors don't have that kind of money. If a company splits itself and the price goes from say, $100 down to $50, more people are likely to become investors, and in turn, this allows existing shareholders more of an opportunity to sell their shares when desired. The more interested shareholders there are, the more liquid the investment becomes. We will talk more about liquidity as an important investment consideration later.

You may wonder if realizing stock splits are important to the successful outcome of an investment. One example of a company that has never split its stock but has still produced phenomenal returns is Warren Buffet's holding company – Berkshire Hathaway. The company began trading publicly in the mid 1950's, but for this exercise, let's just examine the price from the time Buffet actually took over control in 1964, at which time the stock price was approximately $19 per share. Investing $2,000 would have yielded just over 100 shares, so we will keep it at the round lot of 100 for simplicity. Buffet has *never* split the Class-A stock, and so we would expect the price to be quite high – and it is, trading today at $320,500 per share.[16] This easily calculates your total investment to be worth **$3,205,000** today. Using my *time value of money calculator,* it would translate the average annual return to roughly 13.61 percent for over 55 years. Tremendous! If I'm reading your mind correctly, you're wondering why Buffet doesn't ever split his stock. There is one fundamental reason for not splitting shares. He prefers to attract investors who aren't as likely to *trade* the stock, but rather those who are *owners.* A lower share price typically entices short-term investors, even day traders who can cause price fluctuations in the shares via buying and selling.

---

[16] Price as of July 11, 2019

Alternatively, a stock price which has climbed into the thousands of dollars per share will most likely be less affected by the psychological whims of short-term investors.

Which method is better? Both have their pros and cons. Future stock splits should not be a primary consideration for you in your decision making. If they happen, fine. If they don't, that's fine too. You can grow your wealth the same either way. Investing in great companies with growing earnings is your primary consideration.

PROFESSIONAL MANAGEMENT

Finding and investing in the winners early on can be difficult, but with professional management, your odds will likely increase.

For each of the successful corporate growth stories, there are a hundred unsuccessful ones. Attempting to replicate what happened for Apple, Microsoft, or Disney shareholders is filled with risk. It can be difficult to determine which companies will go from small fish to giant fish in 10, 20 or 30 years. I believe corporate management is the biggest factor affecting a company's success, but other issues should also be considered, such as government regulations, competitive positioning, access to capital and public approval, which is critical in our age of social media. A more prudent strategy would be to allocate money across multiple companies and gain more opportunities to find the golden eggs. For those who aren't inclined to study markets, research companies, stay abreast of corporate earnings, and monitor various product launches, which collectively requires many hours per week as well as a lot of skill, I suggest utilizing professionals.

There are thousands of mutual funds available to public investors, and all have specific mandates. A mutual fund is generally very liquid and shares can be purchased and sold any business day. Pricing occurs at the end of trading each day, once closing prices of the collective securities owned by the fund have been accounted. You will be able to find funds that invest in U.S.-based companies, foreign companies, emerging market companies and all types of subsectors in between. There are large, medium, and small company funds, in addition to growth, value, socially responsible and commodity funds. If you're interested in certain sectors, you can invest in technology funds, healthcare funds, financial services funds and utility funds, to name a few.

Finding the right funds and then putting several together to form a diversified portfolio is something that might require the help of an experienced financial advisor. If you're just getting started, however, and you have a long timeframe to invest, choosing a good large cap[17] stock fund is probably a good first step. Adjusting your asset mix during various life stages and for different goals is also important. You don't want short-term goals to be exposed to fluctuations within the equity (stock) market. Longer-term goals should include equities to the extent you are comfortable with the ups and downs of the markets, but another factor to consider is the required rate of return to produce the ending value needed for each goal.

The biggest reason I advocate implementing a *dollar-cost averaging strategy*, whereby a certain amount of money is invested at regular intervals, is because it takes emotion out of the equation. Left to their own free will, people will make unwise decisions when the scales of emotion tip too far to one side or the other. Take a hypothetical guy named Dick, for example. He's a guy who never seems to be on the

---

[17] Large capitalization. Capitalization equals the total number of shares multiplied by the share price. Large cap companies are typically north of $10 billion.

right side of anything and is just too stubborn to accept professional help for things he assumes he's smart enough to handle on his own. I have personally tried to work with a number of clients like Dick early in my career, but I've finally decided these personality types cannot and will not be pleased no matter how well I do for them. Dick is always eager to talk stocks and has lots of ideas to "help" manage his accounts. He is consumed with making money and beating the market. He wants all of the upside in a bull market, as there appears to be *no* risk when stocks are rising. Yet he wants to be on the sidelines when markets hit a rough patch. He expects the advisor to have a crystal ball to tell him when to get out. This, of course, is impossible. Even the veteran professionals can't predict with any accuracy when markets will go up and when they might go down over a short period of time. Unfortunately, Dick doesn't accept this explanation. He's the type of person who doesn't keep his arms and legs inside the ride at all times. He wants to do exactly what his advisors ask him not to do, which is grab the reins and take over control of the wagon when the road gets a little bumpy. He therefore chooses to steer the wagon onto a completely different course. In the market downturn in late 2018 where the S&P 500 dropped close to 20 percent, people like Dick became agitated and angry about market value declines, leading many to the decision to abandon ship with their investment portfolios.

During the recession of 2008, financial advisors largely recommended that their clients stay the course and, if possible, put more money to work during the temporary downturn. But nearly all advisors have dealt with a client like Dick, who insists that he *knows* values are going much lower, thus demanding his accounts be liquidated. Dick is a gauge for many advisors as to when the selling may be over and the market recovery might soon begin. I often talk to other financial advisors who I know and respect, and universally, we all have at least one client with whom we base our contrarian views upon. When he or she finally capitulates and wants to sell, we start to expect the markets will rally. When he or she wants to buy, we feel a market downturn is fast approaching. Dick is the worst kind of investor – one who reacts with emotion rather than relying on the wisdom of long-term investing principles cultivated by the virtues of a capitalistic economic system. When it comes to investing, don't be a Dick!

The emotional roller coaster is very real and needs to be addressed prior to becoming an investor. Furthermore, experienced investors should mentally revisit difficult periods, even if they have been through the cycle dozens of times. The following chart does an excellent job of illustrating how most people feel as the market moves through the various stages of an investment cycle.

Sungarden Investment Management 2018

Notice the *Point of Maximum Financial Opportunity* is depicted by feelings of panic, anger, and depression. The moral of the story – when you feel like throwing up, punching a hole through the wall, or staying in a dark room all day, you may want to ramp up your investment contributions.

Investing can sometimes feel like a lonely walk in the woods. You hear things, start looking around, yelling out for confirmation that you are not alone. It can be scary and nerve-wracking when you hear others bragging that they sold everything and are sitting in stable value funds (money markets) or decided to get out and buy real estate or whatever else is in vogue at the moment. This is the time you need to fall back on your convictions. Remember the tenets of being a successful investor – don't run when others start running. Stick with your plan. Look around at the public companies you and others patronize every day, week or month. Heed the advice of great investing minds.

Be Greedy When Others are Fearful.

There will always
be a easy path and a
right path.

J.K. ROWLING

CHAPTER FIVE

HANG WITH THE RIGHT CROWD

You will likely spend close to half of your life in the workforce and every year is important in your path to prosperity. With that being said, you shouldn't waste time working for a company that holds you back or doesn't treat you fairly. First and foremost, find the type of work that you truly enjoy, and then seek out the employer that offers you the best overall package to perform that work. If you have the right resources and skills, perhaps you will even start your own business at some point. But remember, no matter whether you work for yourself or someone else, the focus should be on the clients or customers. If you can find ways to help your employer win new customers and keep existing ones, you will be considered a key employee and advancement within the organization will be at your fingertips.

At my firm, we don't fall into the typical Wall Street image with designer suits, sports cars and big words. We don't speak in a hard-to-understand lingo. Here, we show up in jeans and button-down shirts. We try to live by the *Code of the West*. This is to say, we understand the value of relationships and hold ourselves to a higher standard than most. We feel we can do what we do every day even without all of the outside forces, rules and regulations to hold us accountable to our clients. Cowboys of the old west handled their affairs with each other in this way – with a sense of pride from doing an honest day's work. The Code called for treating people with respect and carrying out business with authenticity. I chose to partner with Raymond James Financial Services for these precise reasons. After having spent 10 years at two different Wall Street brokerages, I felt I would be better able to serve my clients partnered with a firm which shared my values. The culture at Raymond James could not have been a better fit.

Let me explain how polar opposite some firms' cultures really are. I worked as a financial advisor for a particular Wall Street firm. During that time, the firm was a subsidiary of a financial behemoth which owned bank and lending divisions, asset management businesses, trust and insurance businesses, etc. There were management groups at each level within each organization. The parent company was so big that the smaller divisions it owned were more or less a footnote. Upper management flew around in corporate jets and soaked up fat salaries and healthy stock option bonuses. Those at the top reportedly took lunch each day at the Four Seasons, arriving by limousine.

During my search to find a more suitable custodian/advisory firm, I visited **Raymond James** headquarters in St. Petersburg, Florida. There, I encountered something quite different. After a tour of the offices where I met several department heads, I was invited to lunch by one of the regional managers. The lunchroom at Raymond James is similar to a cafeteria at a high school, complete with lunch trays and plastic plates. While holding my tray waiting to move through the line, I spotted Tom James and Paul Reilly, the former and current CEOs of Raymond James, standing patiently with their own trays in hand.

Seeing this warmed my heart. I knew then that the company was different. The leaders of the entire organization didn't see the need to separate themselves from the "ordinary" rank and file employees, and I was impressed. This cultural attribution is alive and well at Raymond James where the firm's values are placed behind the clients'. Every employee believes that only when they help the firm's clients achieve financial success do they achieve their own.

One thing is for sure – working for the right company is very important in many ways. We talked about the corporate benefits most companies make available to their employees in order to attract and retain quality people. The other factors to consider are culture, freedom to bring your own ideas to the table, advancement opportunities, feeling valued and appreciated, and the little perks like team-building activities or breakroom drinks and snacks. Great employees make great companies. Smart leaders and CEOs know this.

Look at **Southwest Airlines** for example. Employee salaries are competitive and they also offer a valuable profit-sharing plan. The employees rank company culture as one of the most important attributes.[18] **Lululemon** is another company that ranks high in employee satisfaction. According to several employee comments, the company makes the work environment fun, yet they provide for growth within the organization.[19] Employees at **Google** consistently place the company near the top of most admired companies for which to work. The one overriding characteristic for these companies is a positive culture.[20]

---

[18] "Southwest Airlines Reviews." *Glassdoor,* https://www.glassdoor.com/Reviews/southwest-airlines-re-views-SRCH_KE0,18.htm.

[19] "Lululemon Reviews." *Glassdoor,* https://www.glassdoor.com/Reviews/lululemon-Reviews-E42589.htm.

[20] "Google Reviews." *Glassdoor,* https://www.glassdoor.com/Reviews/google-reviews-SRCH_KE0,6.htm.

In your quest to find the right employer, make sure you talk to current and former employees. Get their take on how happy they are to go to work every day. When you find the right company and land a job, set your goals for the title or role you ultimately want to obtain. Most upper-level managers will receive additional perks, such as stock options or employee incentive plans, which usually include bonuses in company stock based on profitability. Receiving annual awards of company stock can short-track your path to millionaire status. Of course, the stock value is all tied to how profitable the company is, so it's important to avoid hooking your wagon to the wrong pony.

CLIMB THE RANKS

No one ever starts out at the top. Well, I suppose the heirs to the kings and queens of the various empires in the world did, but 99.9 percent of people have to pay their dues. There is a path for all of us and it leads as high as we want to keep climbing. Some are capable of soaring to higher peaks in relatively short time frames, while others must clamber along at a slow and steady pace. Starting out in any career, profession or life pursuit, we must accept the fact that we will spend some time in the trenches.

The early trainers I worked for used to send me out in hay fields with barbed wire fences and irrigation ditches to gallop their horses. After all, my home town still has cattle guards at every freeway on and off ramp. Further, I was expected to gallop the rank, unbroken, and ornery horses the more experienced jockeys didn't want to ride. I had horses bolt, buck, run-off and throw me off more times than I can count. In those first few months of learning to gallop racehorses, I definitely had to pay my dues. Once, I had a 2-year-old run-off with me (this is when a horse runs-away at full speed and fails to respond whatsoever to the rider – essentially the horse is in complete control). He was flying through the field toward the fence corner and I knew things weren't going to end well. About 10 feet from the fence line, he ducked back to the left sharply, throwing me straight into the fence, which I hit at 35 miles per hour and rolled into the field ditch. I lay unconscious and didn't wake up until a long time later at my grandpa's house. The trainer found me and simply hauled me there to sleep it off.

Another time, a few months later, I was on a different trainer's horse out in his hay field for a morning gallop. The horse was very full of himself and started to buck when I wasn't prepared. He threw me off after about three jumps and I landed on the rock hard dirt in an awkward angle on my right leg. It snapped at the femur bone. I looked down while I lay in the field and saw my leg lying behind me in a way it shouldn't. All I could do was lift my whip in the air and wave for help. That was the worst pain I had ever felt up to that point in my life. The ambulance finally arrived and the paramedics put a device on my leg to stretch the femur bones out so as to avoid the jagged edges puncturing an artery. I nearly passed out the pain was so intense. I arrived at the hospital, underwent surgery, and was admitted for recovery. Interestingly, my room was two doors down from Dad's room. He was already there, as a patient, healing up from back surgery. He was so pissed that I had agreed to ride horses for that trainer. I didn't, ever again. But I certainly didn't quit my dreams. I was back in the saddle two months later.

To advance in any organization, you need to have a strong work ethic and determination. You can expect to have struggles. The ones who jump up and try again will eventually get over the wall. These are the habits which help you to reach the top:

1. **Stand out from others-** Average isn't good enough. Do things that will get you noticed. For example, posting something thoughtful or even bragging about someone's accomplishments is a great way to build rapport. Everyone likes to see their name in a public place like Facebook or Instagram. Also, make sure you are dressed appropriately for your environment. I strongly recommend paying a little more for high-quality clothing. If you wear nice clothes you will have more confidence, not to mention they will last longer. This doesn't mean to overpay for designer stuff. Just be aware of quality and current styles.

    One morning, I was working a horse for legendary trainer D. Wayne Lukas at Santa Anita back in 1996. I'll never forget what he told me that day as we were riding off of the track and back to the barns. He said, "If you want to be taken seriously and interact with wealthy people, people who can help your career in whatever field you choose, you need to look and act as if you have a million dollars." From that day on, I started to take note of people who were respected and at the top of their professions. Sure enough, nearly all of them portrayed a confident and successful image. I started dressing in nicer clothes and shined my shoes obsessively. This small wardrobe enhancement boosted my confidence a lot. The upgrade in self-esteem was especially important when I traded in my boots and saddle for a briefcase and financial calculator.

2. **Listen more than you talk-** Be curious about other people. Ask a lot of questions. You'll be amazed at how many friends you'll make by doing nothing more than listening to them talk. Remember names and important events. Use calendar reminders to acknowledge people on special occasions, not just birthdays. Think of anniversaries or milestones or even when their favorite team wins. Find out what people are passionate about and make it a point to send them a hand-written note if you learn something exciting pertaining to that part of their life.

3. **Be very careful of your digital footprint-** Anything you post online or send out in social media channels or email will be retrievable. *Forever*. Don't assume you are only talking to your buddy and a crude joke will just be between you two. So many people have lost jobs and even served jail or prison time this way. Aspiring politicians have had their campaigns shattered by just one errant tweet, which may have occurred years prior. The best solution is to just refrain from saying anything which could be considered offensive. Also, avoid engaging in message boards or forums to argue over political or religious or personal choice issues. Those are not places to make your stand unless it will have a direct and meaningful impact on your family or your career. Most online trolls are just looking for a fight and they do so in the comfort of their homes so they don't actually have to speak to someone face-to-face. Don't let yourself get dragged down to the bottom of the barrel.

4. **Build your network-** Do what you can to associate with those who can have a positive influence on your career. This may include people in a role or with a title you would also like to have. It may also include people who have been successful in an area you are pursuing. Most times, these influencers will be older than you. They have vast experience and wisdom to help you avoid costly mistakes, plus they can help you connect with others who can serve as a launch pad for your own aspirations.

5. **Stay in the moment-** You can't control what tomorrow may bring and you can't change what has already happened. Getting all wrapped-up with this type of worrying causes all sorts of *dis-ease*, in the form of mental and physical ailments. Enjoy each moment. Breathe and actually feel yourself breathing. And don't forget to be nice to yourself. Tell the inner critic to take a hike. You are great! God doesn't make mistakes.

Drag your thoughts away
from your troubles…
by the ears, by the heels,
or any other way
you can manage it.

MARK TWAIN

CHAPTER SIX

DEALING
WITH EMOTIONS

S ome people are really good at handling their emotions. Deepak Chopra, the Indian-born American author and public speaker at the forefront of alternative medicine is one. He claims he has not been angry in more than 35 years. How is this possible? First off, he is well grounded in the present moment. He does not let his thoughts run the show. He understands very well that worrying or even overanalyzing what happened in the past and what may happen in the future are of no value.[21] He knows the mind can be both our greatest asset as well as our greatest liability if we let it run wild. How can we become more like Deepak and others who deal with emotions in a Zen-like manner?

---

[21] Oprah. "Deepak Chopra: Creating Harmony." *Oprah's SuperSoul Conversations,* 13 Mar. 2019, https://player.fm/series/series-2372201/deepak-chopra-creating-harmony.

MEDITATION

Keeping your emotions in check is often talked about but is very hard to do, even with the methods I've outlined earlier. Following a mindfulness lifestyle is what I have found to be the single biggest factor in promoting better health, both physically and emotionally. Meditation is becoming very popular, and justifiably so. According to several scientific studies, people who meditate just one minute per day show an actual change in cellular structure in their bodies. Practicing meditation regularly can teach us to be less reactive, and in turn, less likely to make rash decisions or pull the trigger before carefully considering all of the possible outcomes. I have three different meditation apps on my phone and I use all of them. They are full of different meditation practices for different moods or challenging situations with which we may be dealing. Another common, yet simple technique is to use the *breathe* app on your Apple watch or Fitbit. Set it to three minutes or five minutes and sit with your eyes closed, doing your best to focus on nothing but your feelings and senses, such as your breathing or your feet touching the floor or how you feel inside. When you notice yourself thinking about something, let it go and refocus on your senses.

NUTRITION

After spending about eight years on a starvation diet to make the weight limits for a jockey, I wanted to eat real food again. The night I rode my last race at Los Alamitos racecourse and stepped on the scale for the final time of my career, I decided to get even for all of the missed meals I had endured over the years. What did I eat? A foot-long hoagie sandwich from a convenience store, of all things. That was the first sandwich I had eaten in years. It was disgusting but I ate every bite and was sick for hours. A week later, I was sent to New Jersey to attend the two-week broker training for PaineWebber. There were around 60 newly-licensed brokers there, all looking to make it in the financial services industry. We sat in classroom lectures all day and did role playing in the evenings. I hated the sitting around since I was used to being outside all day. One thing I enjoyed, however, was the never-ending supply of food. They fed us tons of food. In that short two weeks, I gained 20 pounds. I was not happy about the transformation, although not enough to back off on the eating. I started to feel depressed and I became overly anxious about my appearance. When I returned home, people couldn't believe how much different I looked and I took that as motivation to begin a better relationship with food. There is a balance within a healthy diet. You really are what you eat.

EXERCISE

Getting your blood pumping several times each week, if not every day, is extremely important to your long-term success. To replace the physical activity of riding, I started running. At first I could only go about a mile, and I didn't like it much. But I found a few guys who ran every morning and somehow I fell into their group. This gave me the accountability factor that is so important in the accomplishment of goals. We would run four or five miles every week-day morning and within a year, I had signed up for a marathon. Since then, I have run in more than 60 marathons, including four Boston Marathons. I have run three 50-mile ultra-races. I also ran the 100-mile Wasatch 100 Endurance Race. This was the most difficult thing I have ever done, taking months of training and a lot of mental fortitude to keep moving through the mountain trails toward the finish. I would have never completed the race without the help of my pacers, Shaun Peterson, Eric Gerdes, and especially my wife, Heather, who kept me going throughout the night when I wanted to quit. She gave me the motivation I needed when my mind began playing tricks on me. My time of 33 hours and nine minutes running that course made me appreciate life in a whole new way. That will always be a memory I can look back on when things seem tough. For anyone seeking a major bucket-list challenge, sign up for a 100-miler!

I much prefer the serenity and tranquility of mountain trail running to road running. Trail running allows me to clear my mind and simply connect with nature instead of thinking so much. Running is a lot like investing. You need to set some long-term goals. You need a plan for how to accomplish those goals. You need good resources. And you need to stay motivated when things don't feel so good. You may not notice results right away, but they definitely show up over time. Plus, both require some initiative to get started. The key is to commit and take the first step.

KEEP A POSITIVE ATTITUDE

We all need to get rid of that critical voice in our head for a while every day. It doesn't matter how it's done, as long as it's legal, relatively safe and it brings you happiness. Watch a game and cheer on your favorite team, read a book, play video games, prepare a meal, talk to a friend, listen to music, do crafts or work on a project. The key is, as often as possible, you need to fill your mind with positive thoughts in order to counteract the worry created by the inevitable forces of life. (For investors, those may include corrections, recessions, and bear markets.) Positive thinking is a highly critical factor in every part of our overall wellness. In order to have financial success, a person needs to have a solid foundation underneath him.

To take it a step further, what good is all the money in the world if you aren't happy with yourself? When we consider employment, sometimes the difference between getting hired and getting passed over has more to do with attitude than skill set. I have spoken with several executives about hiring the right employees and the consensus is, they would rather hire the person who brings energy and a can-do attitude versus the really smart guy who dampens the mood of every room he enters.

To make the best impression on people and to win lots of friends, work on smiling more. Be unique and memorable in an endearing way. People will remember you if you are genuinely interested in them and make them feel important. Shake hands firmly and call people by their names. Don't do this more than once or twice in a conversation, as that becomes awkward at best, and creepy at worst. But do it once, for sure. According to Dale Carnegie, one of the greatest teachers and authors of all time, a person's name is to that person the most important sound in the human language.

FIND THE BALANCE

Think of your mind as having an old-fashioned weighing scale inside – one side for positive thoughts and one side for negative. If you add too many bad thoughts and worries to the negative side, you will be considered an unhappy and a disagreeable person. Your attitude will broadcast outward and cause conflict with family and colleagues. Furthermore, the scale will become so unbalanced that your unconscious mind may eventually inflict physical pain as a mechanism to disguise the undesirable emotion. Not only will you negatively affect those around you, but you will negatively affect yourself.

If you aren't already aware that the mind and body are fully integrated, you should be. The mind is the beginning and the end, the alpha and omega. If the mind is in a negative state too often, it will produce physical symptoms. This often comes in the form of headaches, stomachaches, and illnesses. A few really smart medical and behavioral doctors figured out that these same negative emotions are the real cause of the epidemic of pain syndromes spreading across the civilized world. Back pain, neck pain, joint pain, Fibromyalgia, depression, acid reflux, Crohn's disease, and essentially all of the auto-immune diseases are affecting millions of people in our society, yet mainstream medicine refuses to correlate the problem with our emotional state or the unconscious mind. Most physicians would rather write prescriptions and focus on the symptoms rather than uncovering the root cause. I have a lot of personal experience to share on this topic and I'll write about that in my next book. For now, just know that you shouldn't trust everything you hear from the medical community. Hundreds of thousands of people have figured out how to heal themselves from these and other conditions considered even more serious. Work on your mind and your body will follow. Feel free to email me for more specific information. Contact information can be found at ***www.petersonws.com.***

PREPARE FOR THE UNEXPECTED

Divorce is happening at a high rate in modern times, with many factors playing a role. One of the leading causes of divorce in our country is financial trouble. According to a study done by Forbes magazine in 2019, conflicting money styles is often a source of conflict in marriages. If one person is a saver and one is a spender, continual tension builds in a marriage, often leading to separation or divorce as the final outcome.[22] Deciding to call it quits is becoming a fairly normal option, but from my experience in helping hundreds of clients with their divorce settlements, most people have not considered just how expensive it really is. Assets need to be divided, yet household budgets typically nearly double since each person will need to pay separate utility bills, pay for groceries and other fixed expenses. Legal bills to settle a divorce case are another big drain, as they can reach into the tens or even hundreds of thousands of dollars if the case is highly contested.

If you find yourself considering divorce, stay focused on the critical issues, such as a fair division of assets and income. Further, consider the long-term projections of net worth and net income 5 and 10 years down the road. These projections can lead to a more educated financial settlement in which both parties can start a new chapter in their lives with confidence. For some people entering divorce, women in particular, they can completely lose their identity and ability to move on after divorce. I attribute most of this to being uninformed about the family finances beforehand, thus causing them to freeze up when faced with the decision-making on their own. I try to encourage our female clients to stay engaged and to learn as much as possible about their investments, retirement plans, insurance policies, and sources of income. In this way, they will be much more confident if they ever need to face life as a divorcee or a widow.

---

[22] Shaw, Gabbi. "These Are the 11 Most Common Reasons People Get Divorced, Ranked." *INSIDER,* 31 Jan. 2019, https://www.insider.com/why-people-get-divorced-2019-1.

DON'T PANIC

When market prices fall, the first emotion people experience is worry. They worry that prices will go down even further and their hard-earned investment dollars will be permanently lost. We have to constantly remind ourselves of the investing fundamentals in order to avoid making drastic mistakes in these circumstances. Even though I have addressed this issue several times already, it's important to let this sink in deep.

1) Remind yourself why you are investing. Is it to build your retirement nest egg? Grow funds for a college education? Purchase a vacation home? Go back to the original reason and ask yourself if this is still the goal. If it is, your strategy should remain in place. Prices just got cheaper so seriously consider ramping up your contributions while you can.

2) Avoid getting swept up in the anxiety of the moment. Most financial news outlets experience the largest viewership during periods of high emotion. Fear and hype sell ads. The more fear they can create when markets are falling, the more people will tune in, looking for answers. The advice of so-called experts who appear on television and radio programs telling you to move in or out is quite often bad for your wealth.

3) Check your values only periodically throughout the year. Putting too much emphasis on short-term numbers is a no-no. Values will fluctuate every single day. You must get used to this fact and remain focused on the long-term benefits of your chosen strategy. Would you bench a .300 hitter if he went 0-for-4 in one game?

Certainly not. Let the long-term averages take care of themselves. This doesn't mean you shouldn't stay informed. Have a working knowledge of what's going on in the economy and with the financial markets but keep a level head. Manage your portfolio like a good major-league manager would handle his team, with patience and a steady hand.

4) Stick to it. Nothing good ever came cheap. You have to fight through the desire to give up or to abandon your plan when you feel as if you've made a terrible mistake putting your money in the market in the first place. Just because the prices of your holdings keep going lower doesn't mean everyone else knows something you don't. It most likely just means everyone else has lost their nerve and caved in.

Perseverance is critical. I achieved whatever success I achieved because I was unwilling to stop.

NADIA COMANECI

What is the difference
between a taxidermist and
a tax collector?
The taxidermist takes
only your skin.

MARK TWAIN

CHAPTER SEVEN

HOLD ON
TO YOUR HORSES

For some, the idea of minimizing tax obligations can be mundane and seem uninteresting, but I equate it to reading the directions before setting out to build the playset. (I've built a couple of playsets, and believe me, reading the directions first provides the best end result.) You don't want to just jump in and start nailing things together, because when you screw up (and you will screw up), you will not only have the painful experience of starting over, but you also run the risk of abandoning the project altogether. In the set of instructions for assembling almost anything, there is always a big, bold section stating, *"Warning: Read this before you begin."* With investing, that warning section has to do with taxes. Taxes can take a big bite out of your total investment returns, so it's helpful to look for tax-advantaged strategies whenever possible in building a portfolio. Even further, consider future taxable events before making choices. "Will you be in a higher tax bracket next year?" "Do you have significant capital gains to pay in this tax year?" "Are you going to be losing certain deductions?" Questions like these should be addressed before selling one of your holdings and triggering a large capital gain.

Investment decisions shouldn't be driven solely by tax considerations, but it is very helpful to pay only what is required and to keep the government at bay for as long as possible – sometimes forever!

One of the biggest mistakes I see people make is to offer a free loan to the U.S. Government every single year. You may be doing it right now. What do I mean? Each pay period, your employer will withhold a certain amount of money for federal and state taxes. Oftentimes, people over-fund their tax bill by withholding more than necessary for taxes. Then, when the tax return is filed, they will receive a tax refund for overpayment during the prior year. This seems like a wonderful gift to most folks. The wheels start spinning on how best to spend it. Unfortunately, this is a terrible situation to be in, and one about which I certainly wouldn't be bragging.

First off, the overpaid funds earn no interest for you. The government enjoyed using your money for a full year with no consequences. Second, these funds could have been utilized to increase your investment contributions – a large opportunity wasted. And third, people almost always spend the refund on something that is not beneficial to their wealth. They go on a vacation, buy a new toy or blow it some other way. They treat it as if it were a gift that came out of the blue, when in fact it was their money all along. The solution is to correct any overpayments by adjusting down what your employer withholds. It may be wise to visit with your tax preparer on this matter.

TAX-DEFERRED AND TAX-FREE INVESTMENTS

Tax-deferral is the process of delaying (but not necessarily eliminating) until a future year the payment of income taxes on income you earn in the current year. For example, the money you put into a 401(k) retirement account isn't taxed until you withdraw it, which may be 30 or 40 years down the road!

Tax-deferral can be beneficial because:

1) The money you would have spent on taxes remains invested.

2) You may be in a lower tax bracket when you make withdrawals from your accounts (for example, when you're retired).

3) You may accumulate more dollars in your accounts due to compounding. You remember that concept, right? The Eighth Wonder of the World.

Compounding is so important that I'll explain it briefly again. Compounding means your earnings become part of your underlying investment, and they, in turn, earn interest. In the early years of an investment, the benefit of compounding may not be that significant. But as the years go by, the long-term boost to your total return can be dramatic.

Keep in mind that tax-deferred is not the same as tax-free. *Tax-deferred* means the payment of taxes is delayed, while *tax-free* means no income taxes are due at all. Some savings vehicles such as Roth IRAs are known for their tax-free features. Municipal bonds are an example of an investment that produces income typically tax-free on the federal level, and in many cases also at the state level.

TAX-ADVANTAGED ACCOUNTS FOR RETIREMENT

One of the best ways to accumulate funds for retirement or any other investment objective is to use tax-advantaged (i.e., tax-deferred or tax-free) accounts when appropriate.

■ **Traditional IRAs:** Anyone under age 70½ who earns income or is married to someone with earned income may contribute to an

IRA. Depending upon your income and whether you're covered by an employer-sponsored retirement plan, you may or may not be able to deduct your contributions to a traditional IRA, but your contributions always grow tax-deferred. However, you'll owe income taxes when you make a withdrawal (and a 10 percent additional penalty tax if you're under age 59½, unless an exception applies). As of 2019, Federal law allows for a maximum of $6,000 in total annual contributions. Catchup contribution limits are $1,000 (for those age 50 and over).

■ **Roth IRAs:** Roth IRAs are open only to individuals with incomes below certain limits. Your contributions are made with after-tax dollars, but they will grow tax-deferred, and qualified distributions will be tax-free when you withdraw them. The amount you can contribute is the same as for traditional IRAs. I prefer these accounts over all others if you are eligible. You don't get a tax deduction with dollars going in but the entire account is TAX-FREE coming out if held past age 59½, which could be significant, especially if you have a lot of time on your side to realize those larger doubling balances, as I illustrated previously.

■ **SIMPLE IRAs, SEP IRAs and SIMPLE 401(k)s:** These plans are generally associated with small businesses. As with traditional IRAs, your contributions grow tax-deferred, but you'll owe income taxes when you make a withdrawal. I opened a SEP-IRA during my years as a jockey because the contribution limits are higher than those allowed in a traditional IRA. These plans work very well for self-employed individuals or professionals such as doctors, contractors, and veterinarians.

■ **Employer-sponsored plans — 401(k)s, 403(b)s, and 457 plans:** Contributions to these types of plans are tax-deductible and grow tax-deferred, but you'll owe income taxes when you make a withdrawal. The IRS imposes a mandatory distribution from accounts like IRA's when a person reaches age 70 ½. This is termed an RMD or *Required Minimum Distribution*. This is done to ensure that the government will begin receiving some part of this account value in the form of taxes. With newer plan features of 401(k)s, employers can now allow employees to make after-tax Roth contributions, in which case qualifying distributions will be tax-free.

Now, a word on employment. It is very important that you consider the entire benefit package when you are offered a job with a company. Quite often, new job seekers are only concerned about the hourly wage or monthly salary they will be receiving. After all, this is what they can get their hands on, so it's much more tangible. They don't put much thought into things like health, disability, and life insurance or a retirement plan such as a 401k. Employers with great benefit packages not only offer a 401(k), they provide a *match on the dollars* each employee contributes, typically with a pre-defined limit.[23] A match is free money, yet I see hundreds of employees in my interactions who don't even bother signing up for the plan, so they therefore hand the free money right back. Some businesses are very generous with matching contributions, while others are more conservative. Either way, look for employers who offer these additional benefits. They are a HUGE component of your future wealth profile.

When you sign up for a 401(k) plan, you need to defer as much as possible. Try to put away 10 or 15 percent, if not more. Importantly, don't forget to choose the investments for your deferrals. I have seen far too many participants assume that all they have to do is sign up. This isn't true. The default fund is usually a money market fund that will not allow you to reach the full potential of your retirement. Participants must select their own investments. Choose funds that will

---

[23] Matching contributions from your employer may be subject to a vesting schedule.

coincide with your risk tolerance, and also allow for the best possible returns over time. If you get confused, contact a financial advisor. If all else fails, choose the target-date fund that best matches your expected year of retirement. Target-date funds are a collection of individual funds with a built-in mechanism triggering adjustments to a more and more conservative allocation the closer the date becomes.

■ **Annuities:** With these investments, you pay money to an annuity issuer (an insurance company), and the issuer promises to pay principal and earnings back to you or your named beneficiary in the future. Annuities generally allow you to elect to receive an income stream for life (subject to the claims-paying ability of the issuer). There's no limit to how much you can invest, and your contributions grow tax-deferred. However, you'll owe income taxes on the earnings when you start receiving distributions, and the *earnings* are taxed first with annuity distributions. This is called LIFO accounting (last-in, first-out). I don't recommend annuities for most clients and would never recommend them for a younger person with many years of investment time ahead of them. They are very costly and the fees have a major impact on accumulation over time. They are also difficult to understand, and finally, they are highly illiquid. Annuity companies typically charge surrender penalties for redemptions occurring in less than nine years from the original investment date.

■ **529 plans:** College savings plans and prepaid tuition plans let you set aside money for college which will grow tax-deferred and be tax-free at withdrawal at the federal level if the funds are used for qualified educational expenses. These plans are open to anyone, regardless of income level. Contribution limits are high – typically over $300,000 – but vary by plan. We highly recommend these plans for our clients who want to help their children or grandchildren with educational expenses. If one child decides not to pursue higher education or happens to receive a scholarship, the funds can be easily transferred to a different child without penalty.

Getting started on a college funding plan is an area in which not to procrastinate. College costs keep climbing at an alarming rate. According to the College Board, for the 2018-2019 school year, the average cost of *one* year at a four-year public college for in-state students is $25,890. That is more than the price of a nice car. If you plan on attending a private university, you'll have to get really serious with those contributions, as one year is currently running $52,500 on average. The costs for educating our youth is becoming borderline ridiculous. Some forms of alternative education are cropping up, such as online universities and specialized learning programs, including web-based demonstrations and tutorials. So many students are strapped with debilitating debt loads after finishing college that the U.S. Department of Education has finally taken note. In an effort to help students deal with unnecessary school loans, the department has formed a taskforce to study the massive increase in student debt burdens. Importantly, they made the recommendation that financial literacy courses be required at colleges in order to better educate students on these matters and hopefully give them the necessary tools to avoid sinking so deep into the despair of debt. They also hope to teach students how to develop other financial skills, such as smart investing, budgeting and tax minimization, all of which I'm covering for you in this book.

Though tax considerations shouldn't be your only investing concern, by putting your money in tax-advantaged investment vehicles when appropriate, you'll keep more money in your own pocket and put less in Uncle Sam's. Let's consider the order in which you should allocate your investment dollars:

1) Defer up to the employer's matching contribution amount in your **company-sponsored retirement plan**. This could be 3 percent, 5 percent, or some other value of your salary. In our terminology we say, "Defer up to the *match*." This is technically free money. You're simply crazy if you don't accept it.

2) Make contributions into a **Roth IRA** up to the annual maximum (if eligible). You may contribute to a Roth IRA if you make less than $137,000 as a single tax filer or under $203,000 if you are married, filing jointly. The contribution limits are $6,000 if you're under 50 and $7,000 if you're over. These values are as of 2019.

3) Defer once again into your **company-sponsored retirement plan** up to the annual maximum.

4) If you don't have a company-sponsored plan where you work and you are really looking for tax deductions, open a **Traditional IRA** account in your own name. You will need to have earned income in order to contribute to any IRA.

5) Open a **general investment account** at a reputable investment firm. These accounts are taxable each year so you'll receive a 1099. Pay attention to the investments you choose and try not to sell any appreciated assets with less than a one-year holding period. The IRS classifies investments held under one year as *short-term* gains/losses and the gains are taxed at the ordinary income tax rates. Those held longer than a year are considered *long-term* and are taxed at the more favorable rate of 20 percent or even 10 percent, based on income level.

Don't let the tail wag the dog when it comes to the tax issue. Too often, people choose to invest only if there is a tax benefit in doing so – such as a deduction for an IRA contribution. This thinking is all wrong. You can invest much larger amounts per year in standard investment accounts, and if you have a taxable gain, you obviously made a profit. You only pay tax on the gains and the income each year.

Be aware, however, that with taxable accounts, even if you *reinvest* the capital gains and/or the dividends, you will still pay tax on those amounts each year. Many people don't grasp this concept. Try to think of it like receiving a bonus from your boss which went automatically into your bank account. You never really touched it but it still happened. In the case of dividends and capital gains, you could have taken the cash out of your account and tossed it around on your mattress *or* those dollars could be reinvested to buy more shares. The government doesn't care what you do with the money, they just want their piece of the action. Just because you have to give up a little of that bonus to the tax man doesn't mean you should tell your boss to take his bonus and shove it. The same goes for investing.

Wealthy people invest
first and spend what's left.
Broke people spend first
and invest what's left.

UNKNOWN

CHAPTER EIGHT

SAVING VERSUS INVESTING

There is a big difference between saving money and actually investing it. When you are saving, you generally have a short-term need for those funds, but they should also be the source to turn to for any type of emergency. You'll hear the term *emergency fund*, which is the amount you should have set aside in a savings or money market account to cover six-to-nine months' worth of living expenses. You need to be able to get at that money quickly and easily. Say you had a week from hell – your dog got hit by a car requiring a surgery, you lost your job and you wrecked your truck. If you're prepared, you can turn to your emergency fund in this time of crisis.

Once the crisis fund has been established, you need to get serious about your investment strategy to make your money work for you. I find it baffling why many business owners pile hundreds of thousands of dollars into low-yielding bank accounts. Mostly, I find they are simply lazy. They don't take time to consider the opportunity cost of placing that much money at such a terrible return. Essentially, this is the same as losing money, with current bank rates not even paying as much as the inflation rate. Would they allocate half a million dollars to a new business line that guaranteed them to lose money each year? I don't think so.

For individuals, there are some quick and easy steps to turn saving into investing.

How much can you grow your net worth by cutting out some trivial daily expenses and investing that money instead of spending it? Funny you should ask. I taught a class on that very subject 20 years ago when you could actually buy a Coke *and* a 3 Musketeers® bar for a buck. Yep. Fifty cents was worth something. So here we go. Take the dollar you *didn't* spend each day and invest it in the equity market, $30 each month. After 30 years, you would have invested $10,950 and the value would be $67,814, assuming an annual return of 10 percent. After 40 years, the value would be $189,722.[24]

Today, however, a trendy drink is a Monster or a Rockstar which typically costs around $3 each. So let's take the same example but invest $3 per day instead of $1. Your total investment after 40 years of compounding would be worth $569,167. Are those energy drinks really worth more than half a million dollars? This is significantly more money than most 60-year-olds have socked away for retirement, and it was all possible because you eliminated some unnecessary expenses from your daily routine.

Now, I get it. None of us want to cut out all of the enjoyment in our lives. Sometimes it's the little things that get us through the day with a smile on our faces. After all, if we aren't happy, what good is

---

[24] These calculations are based on hypothetical examples and do not represent an actual investment.

all the money in the world, right? What I'm trying to convey is, there are lots of ways we can be smarter with our daily cash flow. If you feel the need to stop at the convenience store every day, you might want to swap your normal purchases for lower-priced items or maybe cut back on your stops altogether a few days each week. Try to avoid impulse spending and get into the habit of asking yourself if your purchases are actually *needs* or simply *wants*.

Make it a part of your weekly habits to monitor how much you have in your various accounts. These days, most people do their banking on smartphone apps. Investment firms also have handy apps that anyone can open up quickly to check balances, performance, account activity, and so on. Just get in the habit of paying attention. *Save* the dollars necessary for running your life or your business in the short-term, but beyond that, attempt to invest and get a better return. Investing is for the longer-term goals and should be funded initially in a lump sum and thereafter using the dollar-cost averaging techniques I referred to earlier. The further away the goal is, the more aggressive you can likely be with your investment choices.

There are times in life when taking risk is appropriate, and even necessary, in order to reach your dreams. When crossing a river by jumping from rock to rock, you can't advance to the next one without leaving the safety of the one you are standing on. This is a calculated risk and the type in which you have some degree of confidence in the outcome. Careers are often made by just jumping in and going for it. I believe there is a universal force that listens to our inner thoughts. If you believe enough in your own success, the universe will see that you achieve it. Before Jim Carrey became Jim Carrey, he vowed that he wanted to hit the big time in acting. He wrote himself a check for $10 million for *"Acting Services Rendered"* and gave himself three years to achieve it. He packed the check around in his wallet everywhere he went as a reminder to the universe. Shortly before the third year was up, he landed the lead role in *Dumb and Dumber* and earned $10 million for the part.

On the other hand, if you incessantly tell yourself you're no good, you won't be. Tell yourself you're a winner, or tell yourself that you're a loser – either way, you're right. I've read stories about people who fretted so frequently thinking they were going to die at a certain age of a certain illness that those fears came true.

INVESTING VERSUS SPECULATING

The younger you are, the more aggressive you can be in life and with your investments. When I say *more aggressive* with investing, I am referring to the allocation of stocks, bonds and cash. I am not referring to speculating in penny stocks or jumping all into one sector or even buying options. Stick with what has worked over decades. Don't go chasing rainbows just because some "really smart guy" sold you on a foolproof investment plan. Traveling the road to riches in a race car is the choice of transportation many will choose. People like the idea of getting rich quickly. Why do you think there are so many Ponzi schemes out there?

What I'm trying to tell you is that the better choice is to take the route allowing you to appreciate the scenery as you pass along. You'll likely enjoy the ride much more and not run the risk of wiping out around every curve in the road. If it sounds too good to be true, it most often is. Settle in with the slow and steady, even when the pull of greed gets strong. You will be tempted to jump into unknown waters because you see coworkers, friends and neighbors profiting from whatever investment boom is taking place.

Go back to the fundamentals. Isn't that what all good coaches say when an athlete is scuffling? There will be times when the best option you can choose for your wealth is to do absolutely nothing. Remember, to win, you must have your focus on the long-term and not the hype from month to month or year to year. Be the tortoise and not the hare.

You can come from humble beginnings, live frugally, invest as much as you can, save 10% to 20% of your paycheck, invest in low-cost ETFs, and become a millionaire.

DAN LaSALLE

OLNEY CHARTER SCHOOL'S ASSISTANT PRINCIPAL

My formula for success is rise early, work late and strike oil.

J.P. GETTY

CHAPTER NINE

APPROPRIATE INVESTMENTS

S tocks are great investment vehicles for the long-term. Millions of people have become extremely wealthy by simply investing in our capitalist economy and holding on. Trends come and go, as do new methods of buying stock. Day trading was all the rage in the late 1990's and early 2000's. That proved to be a fallacy for countless dreamers. Hedge funds, which look to find hidden gems or uncover new methods to screen out winning businesses, have risen in popularity in recent years, only to have subsequently fallen out of favor *again*. The bottom line is, stocks are the asset of choice because they are liquid (an asset that can be readily converted into cash), and as long as the company is publicly traded, anyone can purchase shares. The next question becomes, how should you go about buying stock?

LIQUID AND LOW-COST

The most common method of owning stocks for individual investors is via mutual funds. There are thousands upon thousands of mutual funds registered to operate in our country, so picking the right one can be frightening. What you are looking for is a well-established fund company. This is the administrator and distributor of the actual fund. Fund companies typically offer dozens of different fund choices with different objectives, each having a separate manager or management team. The fund manager or managers are responsible for choosing the individual securities which will be purchased by the fund. A single fund may own more than 1,000 different securities. The more concentrated funds may own 50 or so. Open-ended mutual funds are available for purchase each day at the net asset value. This is the calculated value of the fund officially reported at the end of the day. Investors own shares in the fund and will see their values increase or decrease based on the underlying investments and the internal expenses incurred by the fund.

Exchange Traded Funds (ETFs) are another option. They are similar to mutual funds except they are purchased and sold as if they were regular stocks on stock exchanges. Typical ETFs are more indexed based, so they are built to mirror a specific index, such as the S&P 500 or Russell 2000 or NASDAQ. There isn't an active fund manager making decisions as to the buying or selling of securities for the fund. The holdings are selected and permanently set in place. It is a truly passive strategy, and as such, the costs are lower. To put this into a different context, think of taking a transcontinental flight. You have two options. 1) Fly with autopilot and get a cheaper ticket or 2) Pay more for your ticket and have the captain and co-captain along for the trip. With technology in planes today, you'll likely be fine flying on autopilot. In the event a major storm comes up, you may want to have the captain in the cockpit. There isn't a strong case to be made for which type of fund is better, but you definitely want to pay attention to the cost associated with each. Some people like to have active management for most of their holdings but will also utilize ETFs for filling in areas that look attractive at various times. Others prefer ETFs as their sole investment vehicle due to lower cost and more tax efficiency. Many of the largest mutual fund families also offer ETF's.

No matter which type of vehicle you choose, you'll want to look for a fund that has a long-term performance history which ranks in the top 25 percent of its peer group overall. You shouldn't get carried away choosing the number one performer over a one-year period, as last year's winners will often become this year's losers. You don't want to chase short-term performance only to have dramatic underperformance just a little while later. What usually causes this fall from grace is the fund manager places big bets on specific stocks or sectors and gets it right for a while. But sooner or later, those big bets fall apart, when valuations shift back to normal. Look for funds with solid numbers that hold up over longer periods of time, such as 5-, 7- and 10-year average returns.

There are other asset categories in which to invest, but none offer as much combined long-term growth potential and liquidity as stocks. That includes real estate, when using cash-on-cash comparisons and not leveraging up (borrowing) to make the investment. I will discuss real estate more in-depth coming up. For this discussion, we will stay focused on the more liquid asset classes (those that can be bought and sold easily and typically within minutes or seconds of a trade offer being placed). Here is a chart illustrating the long term REAL returns of the most common asset categories from the year **1802** through **2015**. Real returns are the total return after the effects of inflation are subtracted.

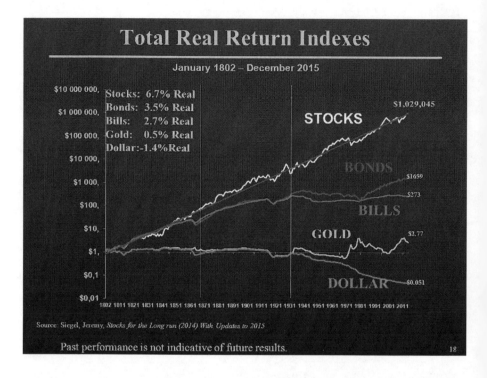

As you can see, gold has barely kept its original value since 1802 and the U.S. dollar has declined by an average of 1.4 percent per year. One dollar invested in bonds would have grown to $1,659 in those 200+ years. The same $1 invested in stocks, however, grew to over $1,029,045. This is dramatic. Additionally, of course, there would have been a good amount of interest paid during those years from bonds, and a sizeable sum of dividends paid from stocks.

The next chart shows the growth of $1 for various asset classes from 1926 to 2017, but it doesn't subtract inflation from the returns. You can make that comparison on your own by noting that inflation itself averaged 2.9 percent per year during that stretch. Essentially, this means that if you didn't earn at least 3 percent per year over that 91-year period, you lost value. Treasury Bills, considered one of the safest and most reliable investments, barely produced a positive return after subtracting the inflationary impact. The cost of goods and services climbs higher and higher every year. If your money is buried in coffee cans for 15 years, you'll have to dig up two cans to purchase what one can used to buy.[25]

Ibbotson® SBBI®
Stocks, Bonds, Bills, and Inflation 1926–2016

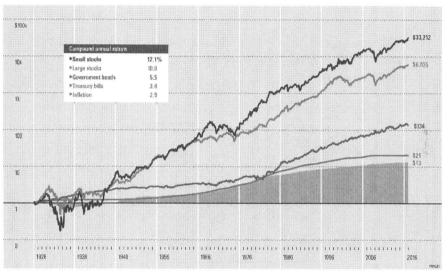

Past performance is no guarantee of future results. Hypothetical value of $1 invested at the beginning of 1926. Assumes reinvestment of income and no transaction costs or taxes. This is for illustrative purposes only and not indicative of any investment. An investment cannot be made directly in an index. ©2017 Morningstar, Inc. All Rights Reserved

By investing in stocks, you stay way ahead of inflation over time and your purchasing power keeps rising. Notice further that this chart separates small companies from large companies and as you might expect, smaller companies do outperform over time. While they pose more risks, the rewards are greater overall. Every company starts out

---

[25] ©2018 Morningstar, Inc. 2018 Fundamentals for Investors PowerPoint. *Stocks, Bonds, Bills, and Inflation® (SBBI®) Yearbook*, by Roger G. Ibbotson and Rex Sinquefield, updated annually.

as just an idea or a concept, which can be considered small on the grand stage. If that idea or concept becomes mainstream, then that company will grow from small, to medium, to large in size and the shareholders will profit every step of the way.

You can't catch the big fish by skimming the surface.

ANDY GILBERT

Starbucks was just a single coffee bean store established in 1971 in Pike Place Market, downtown Seattle, WA. Howard Schultz began working for the company in 1982 and soon formulated the idea to serve great coffee and have friendly baristas in a comfortable, welcoming environment. He left the company in 1985 to start a different chain and then with the help of some other investors, Schultz purchased Starbucks in 1987 and began the iconic franchise we all know today. This single store has now grown into more than 20,000 stores worldwide. Starbucks (SBUX) didn't go public until 1992, 21 years after the Pike Place store opened for business. The IPO price was $17 per share. Assuming you were fortunate enough to buy 100 shares of SBUX at the IPO price for a total investment of $1,700, you would have averaged over 26 percent per year on that investment. SBUX has split its shares two-for-one, six times. This means your original 100 shares would have now become 6,400 shares. At a current market price of $84.30,[26] your initial $1,700 total investment made just 27 years ago would now be worth $539,520.

---

[26] Price as of June 24, 2019

If you like Walmart, this one's for you – or if you don't, maybe you will after reading this. Walmart (WMT) went public in 1972 – coincidentally the year I was born. WMT began trading at $16.50 per share so let's assume Mom and Dad bought me 100 shares of Walmart as a birth gift (which they didn't). Walmart split its stock 11 times since going public – each time at a two-for-one rate. The share progression looks like this:

100 > 200 > 400 > 800 > 1,600 > 3,200 > 6,400 > 12,800 > 25,600 > 51,200 > 102,400 > 204,800 shares

Believe it or not, I would now be the proud owner of 204,800 shares worth **$22,781,952**.[27] That is not a misprint. The $1,650 investment is now worth over $22 million and I haven't even mentioned how many millions of dollars' worth of dividends I would have collected along the way. For perspective, just consider that Walmart currently pays $2.12 annually per share in dividends to shareholders. The total dividends for me in 2019 alone would equal $434,176. Thanks Mom and Dad! What a gift! I sure wish it had actually happened!

Notice the difference in the Walmart ending value versus the Starbucks ending value. $22,781,952 versus $539,520. The main issue here is *time*. To be exact, Walmart has been public 20 years longer than Starbucks. For you sports fans who have ever watched a close-scoring Utah Jazz basketball game on television, you know what Craig Bolerjack says near the end of the fourth quarter, "Buckle up, everybody." So, I'll do the same and tell you to strap in before you read any further, because in my mind, this is even more thrilling! Take the same average annual return Starbucks has delivered to its shareholders of 23.78 percent per year since its IPO and calculate that

---

[27] Price as of June 24, 2009

for *another* 20 years so we would have the same holding period as Walmart (46 years) – $539,520 compounded at 23.78 percent for an additional 20 years equals **$38,460,412.**

No one can predict what annual return Starbucks will deliver to its shareholders over the next 20 years or even the next one year. It may be much less than the average of the first 27, but the fact remains, excellent companies have historically grown their revenues, which in turn rewards their shareholders. Compounding investment earnings is not rocket science. It is a way for people of all walks of life to harness their wealth without backbreaking physical work or any type of advanced degree necessary.

If you aren't getting excited about this stuff, I would advise immediately scheduling an appointment with your physician to make sure your heart is still beating. Everyone gets excited when they win. Have you ever seen a person upset when their name is pulled out of a hat for a prize? Would you be annoyed or disappointed if you found out that you had inherited $100,000 from an elderly neighbor? People may act like money doesn't mean anything, but it's pretty easy to see how they truly feel if they are in the mix for a large payout – or even a tiny one. Watch what people will do for a $20 bill when offered it on a dare. People act like complete morons attempting to catch a free T-shirt thrown up into the stands at a sporting event. Let's all start behaving like that when we're dealing with serious stuff, such as our retirement accounts.

One further point on this. You don't need to purchase shares at the IPO price to become wealthy over time. I could show dozens of examples of buying shares years after the initial offering date, or buying shares in mutual funds and holding those shares over a long time frame with similar results. These examples are merely for illustrative purposes of buying and owning stocks for the long-term and how ownership in great companies can offer substantial rewards.

REAL ESTATE

Many people believe investing in real estate is far safer and more profitable than stocks. While I don't at all agree with that premise, I do recommend having some real estate as a diversification strategy in your overall net worth. For most people, their home is one of their largest assets. The residential home has long been known to provide comfort and a great feeling of security for families. What most people don't realize is, home prices don't appreciate all that fast – usually in the range of 3-4 percent per year.

Why do so many people rave about real estate, then? For the most part, they are misinformed about the true returns. Real estate investing usually involves leverage, so the returns may become enhanced when values go up, and at the same time, returns can be amplified to the downside if values fall. Investing in real estate is ordinarily done for income benefits in the form of rent or lease payments. We calculate the rate of return based on the outlay of capital required to take ownership of the property, also known as cash-on-cash return. It is calculated by dividing the income earned by the equity in the property. In other words, the debt is removed from the equation. Using leverage can amplify the return because less cash is actually needed from the investor to generate the income. This allows for a nice return on invested capital. But there are risks to borrowing – just ask anyone who lost their home in the 2007-2008 real-estate collapse.

Let me try to explain how this works. Assume you decide to buy a $300,000 home and put down the standard 20 percent of your own money, borrowing the other 80 percent from the bank. You have $60,000 invested (300,000 x .20), yet control a $300,000 asset. Now let's assume you live in the home for five years and decide to sell because you need a bigger yard. The home appreciated and you sell for $400,000. For simplicity, we will assume you still owe $220,000 to the bank ($20,000 was applied to the principal of the original $240,000 loan during your five years of making payments). We will also assume you paid the standard 6 percent in real-estate commissions and closing costs. So what is the return on this investment?

$400,000 proceeds

- $220,000 loan payback

= **$180,000**

- $24,000 commissions

= **$156,000 Gross**

Your $60,000 original investment more than doubled in value and you are now getting back $156,000 in just five years. Sounds like a no brainer right? And this is why people incorrectly assume real estate is a sure thing. So far, we have only calculated the gross return as being 160 percent, but you must consider several other factors to get to the *net* return. When you borrow money, there will be an interest charge. The monthly payment largely goes toward paying that interest, especially in the early years of the mortgage. Over a 30 year period, a $240,000 mortgage at an interest rate of 4.5 percent will end up requiring $437,777 of payments. This means the bank will collect $197,776 in interest payments on your original loan of $240,000. OUCH!

So back to the scenario – monthly principal and interest payments would be approximately $1,216.00. This totals $72,960 over the five years. We already subtracted out the principal reduction of $20,000, so the remainder of $52,960 went toward interest. We must remove that money from gross proceeds because it was a cost of owning the home.

$156,000
- $52,960
= **$103,040**

We also forgot to consider property taxes, of course. Assume you paid $3,400 per year to local property taxes on your home. This totals $17,000 over five years. Remove that from profits.

$103,040
-$17,000
= **$86,040**

And now we must consider the maintenance costs over the course of ownership. Things need to be fixed, cleaned, and cared for. Yards need to be kept up. Home ownership isn't a free activity. Therefore, let's assume a modest $200 per month for home-maintenance costs, totaling $12,000 over the five years.

$86,040
-$12,000
=**$74,040**

Finally, you must remember that you put down $60,000 to purchase the home. Your net proceeds of $74,040 less the original

$60,000 outlay equals **$14,040** – this is your *net return,* equating to around 4.2 percent per year. (We haven't even considered the cost of insuring the home over that period of time.) This is closer to the actual experience for homeowners, yet most people will cling to the idea that they hit a homerun with $156,000 of proceeds from the sale. As the late Paul Harvey used to say, "Now you know the rest of the story."

This same illustration can be applied to investment property such as commercial buildings, rentals, etc. You will just need to net out the rental income versus any debt payments in your calculation of return on investment. Owning commercial and rental buildings will also typically require you to purchase insurance such as fire, theft, and general liability in order to protect yourself in the event of an accident or mishap on your property. Drawing up lease contracts is another possible expense, as you will likely need a qualified attorney to handle those issues. And finally, you can't make money unless your building is occupied, so you'll need to keep tenants paying at all times. Don't get me wrong – some real-estate investments have been wildly profitable. People who know what they are doing and purchase properties on the back of the bank's extended credit can make quite handsome profits – especially if they can limit their further out-of-pocket expenses, such as maintenance and upkeep, and if they can keep the building occupied with lease payments arriving on time. I am simply highlighting important factors for you to consider when making investment decisions.

There are also some attractive tax benefits for owning real estate, such as depreciation and certain business activity-related deductions. The drawback for those tax incentives is a near complete loss of liquidity. Selling 5 percent of your real estate quickly, because you need cash for something else, isn't an option. Selling 5 percent of your mutual fund holdings can be accomplished on any given day in which markets are open. Customizing distributions to meet your required lifestyle is also much easier with mutual funds.

And that begs the question, when should you sell?

> It frees you from doing things you dislike. Since I dislike doing nearly everything, money is handy.

GROUCHO MARX

CHAPTER TEN

WHEN
TO SELL

S o far, I hope you have realized reaping the benefits of stock ownership requires buying and holding. Up to now, there isn't much selling going on. But obviously, we will want to start drawing on our investments at some point, right? We aren't simply playing a game to see how much we can accumulate (although I think some people do). There are basically five reasons to sell:

1) Rebalancing: I advocate a regular rebalancing program within your mutual fund and stock portfolios to keep target risk exposure in line with each objectives and risk profile.[28] This serves to help keep your emotions in check. Essentially a portfolio rebalance will trim those holdings that have crept above the target percentage and buy any holdings, which may have fallen below their target percentage. Therefore, you are automatically engaging in selling high and buying low.

---

[28] Rebalancing a non-retirement account could be a taxable event that may increase your tax liability.

2) Goal Funding: Shares must be sold to pay for scheduled or planned goals such as college, a vacation home or retirement. Ideally, the shorter-term goals would be invested less in stock and more in fixed income or bonds. Retirement isn't a one-time event. It lasts for 30 or 40 years and longer. Distributions from a diversified portfolio should be carefully planned out with an advisor and/or tax professional to avoid additional tax obligations and also to sell assets at favorable times with regard to price and outlook. When liquidating from a portfolio, it's a good strategy to use the dollar-cost averaging approach again. This time, however, you will be *selling* at regular intervals rather than buying. If you find yourself in an equity market correction of 10 percent or more, you may consider liquidating more of your fixed income and alternative fund positions rather than selling stock funds. Consider holding onto the equity funds for a few months and allow the market a chance to recover. It may not recover right away, but at least you will be limiting the amount you are selling when prices are low. Remember — it's better to sell high, so the reverse is true if the markets experience tremendous gains. Consider selling a few months' worth of distributions from your equity holdings in anticipation of those future withdrawals.

3) Valuation: If prices of certain assets get inflated and you are having a difficult time justifying the price, it may be time to trim back or even sell that component of your portfolio all together. Technology stocks around the turn of the century would be a good example. They had soared higher and higher over the previous five or six years, and many were trading at unsustainable levels. If valuations get ahead of themselves, you can avoid some level of pain by coming out of the arena and waiting for the dust to settle. This isn't an easy task. Nobody really knows when prices peak or when they bottom. If or when you decide to move capital out of the markets for valuation purposes, I strongly advise to do so slowly – say 5 percent per month for three to six months and I also advocate *not* selling out of your entire portfolio completely. If you had originally invested 20 percent of your portfolio in large cap technology stocks and five years later they had grown to 40 percent, it would not be a bad idea to at least trim back to the original 20 percent or perhaps even scale back further in the technology sector for a while and re-allocate into an area that has better valuations. You may have taxable gains, so always consider the tax impact before making any such decisions.

Prices rise and fall and stocks and sectors move according to investor psychology which can sometimes get really wacky. This shouldn't be your main concern. Invest in great companies and in general, sit tight.

I never attempt to make money on the stock market. I buy on the assumption that they could close the market the next day and not reopen it for five years.

WARREN BUFFET

Markets can change quickly, yet they can also continue on their chosen path for much, much longer than you think. You may find you're out on an island all alone if you go against the direction of the market. Humans are herd animals, so they like the comfort of being with others. In investing terms, this means we seek confirmation of our decisions based on what others are doing. But just like clockwork and after enough time, those standing alone usually cave in and join the crowd. This is how most people make their biggest mistakes. It's called **capitulating**, which means giving into or succumbing to your emotions. It can occur both in a bear market when everyone is selling and thus you decide to as well, and also in a bull market when everyone keeps buying so you jump in, too. Warren's *Second Rule for Success* is this: *Don't base your decisions on what everyone else is saying or doing.*

When he began managing money in 1956 with $100,000 from a handful of investors, people thought he was an oddball. He worked in Omaha, Nebraska, not on Wall Street and he would not provide details on which investments he was making for the investors. People predicted he would fail, but when he closed his partnership 14 years later, it was worth more than $100 million. The path less traveled is your friend, so stay on it and keep your calm.

4) Performance: Monitoring performance can be tricky. I've had many clients who wanted to compare their portfolio performance to that of the S&P 500. This comparison would be fine if they had 100 percent of their portfolio invested in U.S.-based large-company stocks. But 99 percent of clients don't have all of their money invested that way. They will own pieces of mid-size, small-size, international and emerging market companies. They will most often own bonds and money market funds and perhaps some alternative funds such as real-estate or commodities. The S&P 500 is an index of the 500 largest U.S.-based companies and it is *market-cap weighted* which means that the larger companies have a bigger impact on the performance of the index than the smaller ones do. Take the largest company in the United States by market capitalization, Apple, for example. It represents approximately 4.2 percent of the index whereas Nike represents just .44 percent.[29] So comparing an entire portfolio to that single index is unfair and very misleading.

---

[29] Data as of June 24, 2019

Performance should absolutely be considered, as businesses often fall out of favor or fail to keep up with consumer demands. Kodak is a great example of this. For many years, the company dominated the photography industry, but they made a huge error in underestimating the move to digital film and pictures and therefore their competitors virtually destroyed them. Other examples of companies that didn't adapt or failed to innovate include Nokia, Xerox, Blockbuster, Yahoo, JC Penney, AOL, Motorola, Polaroid and Atari. Having superior management is critical for companies not only to thrive, but to survive. If you find yourself owning a company that is underperforming its peer group, look closer. Is there something wrong with the fundamentals? Does the company management have a clear direction of where they are going, which business lines will add value, and who their target customers are? Are they scrambling to keep up with competitors or are they borrowing more and more money to stay afloat? These are some of the red flags that may be telling you to move on.

If your fund is underperforming for extended periods of time – say five or more years – you should consider an alternate fund that has shown a more promising track record. If you have an advisor, he or she likely will have already discussed these problems and will have a plan to deal with them. Usually, you can give proven fund managers a little more latitude, because they are more likely able to right the ship through a storm.

Sometimes we realize we just made a bad decision. Most every investor will have a few mistakes in his or her lifetime. The key is to learn from them. A long-time portfolio manager and partner of a decades-old fund family maintains an entire office hallway adorned with his mistakes so as not to forget. Old stock certificates of companies he purchased for his fund that produced ugly losses, or even went out of business, are placed in a plaque and hung on the wall. He doesn't want to make the same errors in analysis over and over.

Personally, I have made several regrettable investments. I made the wrong call on WorldCom, Enron, and Lucent Technologies, all on the advice of my former brokerage firm's research analysts. I didn't spend enough time doing my own research to make a more informed decision. Each of those companies are now out of business, and two of them were charged with investment fraud. I didn't continue to hold these all the way into the ground. I reassessed the company valuations and projections quite often. Once I felt management didn't have a solid strategy to regain shareholder value, I cut my ties. Don't fall into the trap of thinking you'll hold until the share price gets back to what you paid and then you'll sell. This is a fool's game. If the company is stumbling badly and losing to competitors, it may be a good idea to cut your losses and look elsewhere. Sitting and hoping are not good investment decisions. Good companies that adapt, will most often recover from setbacks. The trick is in knowing the difference.

One thing I see some investors do in these cases of cutting bait (realizing losses) is deciding to give up and get out completely. They make that decision based on that one instance. They are done with investing and plan to never do it again. Luckily for me, I learned at a very young age that if you get bucked off, you jump up and get right back on the horse. I took this advice literally starting when I was 4 years old, and it's carried with me through my entire riding career and spilled over into my investing strategy, as well.

One day at Ruidoso Downs, I was on a horse for the third race of the day in the pre-race warmups, galloping alongside of the pony rider. The horse I was on was young and ill-mannered and threw me off, stepping on my leg after I landed. I felt like I was okay, but track policy requires jockeys be sent by ambulance to the emergency room in such situations. Once at the ER, I was forced to strip down and put on one of those ridiculous gowns that shows your backside. I was very annoyed by the amount of time it was taking the doctor to arrive to examine me. My main concern was to get back to the racetrack because I had what I believed was a sure winner to ride in the fifth. I asked my wife at the time to go out and pull the car up to the entrance. I peeked out of the room and made sure no one was looking, then made a dash through the hallway, past the nurses' station, and through the waiting area filled with other patients and family members (yikes), and then out across the ambulance entrance area and into the car. She sped me back to the racetrack, where I jumped out and ran across the infield in my hospital gown to the jockey's room, flashing my rear end to all of the spectators in the grandstands. Yep, I made it in time to ride a filly named Mildly Sinful in the fifth race and yes, we won the race. What is the moral of this story? If you get thrown off course by one bad incident and you feel like grabbing your marbles and going home, pick yourself up and get back in the saddle. Focus on your other holdings and how they may give you some comfort – even if you feel like your bare ass is completely exposed for a while.

Life is hard.
It's harder
if you're stupid.

JOHN WAYNE

CHAPTER ELEVEN

AREAS
TO AVOID

Every year, more than 30 million people become victims of investment fraud. The average loss is around $15,000, with some more affluent individuals realizing losses well into the millions of dollars. Fraudsters are everywhere, and they are very skilled at glazing up the donut, I'll call it. Many have such a smooth sales approach they could sell milk to a dairy farmer. In the financial services industry, regulators are doing everything they can to crack down on corruption, scams and investment fraud. Reputable firms are required to comply with federal laws administered by the Securities and Exchange Commission (SEC) and Financial Industry Regulation Authority (FINRA). Every registered advisor must meet annual continuing education requirements, as well as complete an in-office audit from a licensed compliance officer. We are highly-regulated on what we can say, what we can email, and how we engage with our clientele. Regulated advisors are prohibited from having any personal access to client funds or to prepare any statements on client accounts;

thus, all client assets must be held in custody by a licensed broker/dealer. These days there is a higher level of accountability for financial advisors than ever before. A new Department of Labor guideline known as the fiduciary standard has been implemented for advisors with regards to customer care. This is a rule requiring fiduciaries to put the clients' interest ahead of their own. Alarmingly, some advisors don't adhere to this policy, but continue to focus primarily on selling products rather than concerning themselves with a client's well-being. When seeking an advisor, I would recommend asking whether he or she holds out as a fiduciary.

Unfortunately, not all investment venues are regulated, and many are created for the sole purpose of stealing money from unsuspecting consumers. The following are stories based on real-life examples, although the names have been changed out of respect for the individuals involved.

One real-life example happened to a lady named Marjorie, an 82-year-old widow. A scammer called and convinced her she had won a sweepstakes prize and that she would simply need to pay the taxes and fees to collect her winnings. Once he had her on the hook, the scammer continued to call with further requirements and conditions, each of which required further payment. In the end, Marjorie lost her life savings – hundreds of thousands of dollars. Feeling profoundly embarrassed and now faced with the prospect of needing to borrow from her family and children to get by, Marjorie committed suicide.

I know of an elderly lady named Diana who is a hairstylist and makes about $30,000 per year. She had worked with my mom at a salon once, so she knew of me. Diana called me about 10 years ago to tell me she had invested some money in a company offshore and had now, a year later, received word that her $5,000 investment was worth millions. The contact person told her she would just need to send in money for the selling-fee and regulatory paperwork to process her check. She sent in those payments and wanted to learn more about how to invest her millions. Seeing how excited and convinced she was that her wise investing decision had paid off, I didn't have the heart to rain on her parade. I simply told her to be careful and left it at that. Another year went by and Diana called again saying the investment had gone up even more and they were just deciding the timing to begin paying everyone off. She said it was just a matter of a few weeks and she would be receiving close to $5 million. When presented with concerns from those around her regarding the "investment", she would often end such conversations abruptly, failing to acknowledge the warning signs. I don't know if she was more embarrassed or simply so entrenched in the lie that she couldn't accept the fact that such an investment scenario was totally ludicrous.

One day about two years ago, I was out working in my horse pasture fixing some fencing when my dad called. He was in a complete panic and started rambling on that my son Cade was in jail and was too afraid to call and tell me so he called my dad, his grandpa. This startled me, as Cade is not the kind of kid to get into trouble with the law. I asked Dad what had happened. He didn't have very many details, but told me some attorneys had called him with Cade on the line to explain that Cade had been busted for drugs and was in jail. The charges would be significant and would go on his record, but there was a way to avoid that if Dad would send in some money to cover his bail. They wanted his credit card. It would only require $2,500 to get him released. Fortunately, Dad called me to find out what to do instead of pulling out the card. He was fully convinced that he had heard Cade on the phone crying and begging for help.

"Grandpa, please don't tell Dad. Just give them your credit card so I can get out of here and I'll pay you back."

He told "Cade" that he would just drive down to the police station and bring a check. (My dad isn't big on credit cards — he's a farmer. Remember?) When he told me the full story, I immediately knew something was not right. I called Cade. He was exactly where he said he'd be – camping with some friends. He was also shocked when I told him about the call. Bottom line is, my dad was the victim of a phone scam geared toward grandparents. It is a very successful scam, since the grandparent thinks he/she is hearing one of their grandchildren plead for help. Most grandparents would do most anything for their grandchildren. Be careful out there. Scammers are tricky and they are great at adapting in order to fit into family situations.

The general tenets of a scam are as follows:

- An opportunity which sounds too good to turn down
- A situation which creates fear
- A situation which creates urgency
- A relationship that preys on loneliness

Consider investments carefully and don't participate in fads, fascinations or schemes. Some people treat stock investing as if it were a Las Vegas slot machine. They incorrectly assume that it's all a game of chance. Peter Lynch, the famed fund manager, said it best with his important quote, "Although it's easy to forget sometimes, a share is not a lottery ticket. It's part ownership in an actual business." He also famously stated, "Invest in what you know." I have found this advice to be very beneficial. Consider where you and your family spend your time and money. Which products or services do you frequently purchase? These observations may be a starting point for an investment decision. Essentially, consider investing in companies that sell products that are useful and popular. Don't take risks with unknowns.

I learned this lesson the hard way one morning at Los Alamitos Racetrack. It was almost 10:00 a.m., time for the track to close from the morning workouts. A relatively unknown Quarter Horse trainer came hustling up to the track entrance where I was coming off with the horse I had just worked out. He was leading a young horse that had never received an official gate workout and asked me if I would be willing to blow her out of the gate. Looking around, I noticed no other riders were available, and even though I didn't know much about this trainer's abilities with Quarter Horses, nor did I know anything about this particular filly, I agreed to do it (mostly because I felt bad for him).

I warmed her up and rode her back behind the starting gates to be loaded. The gate handler slid a lead rope through the D-ring on her bit and began leading her toward the gate. The filly didn't want any part of the starting gate and began fighting the handler. She backed up a few steps and then, without any warning, reared up on her hind legs and flipped herself completely over backwards, landing directly on top of me — flattening me like a pancake. She got up and ran off unharmed. I, on the other hand, lay motionless writhing in pain. I couldn't move. The air wouldn't enter my lungs for what seemed like several minutes. I nearly blacked out from the pain. I was just conscious enough to feel it all.

Once at the hospital, doctors rushed me into the imaging room for X-rays. I couldn't feel my legs and they warned me that I might be paralyzed from the waist down. They would know more once the images were developed. Lying motionless on the gurney, I contemplated my future and how scared I was to face the reality of being a paraplegic. When they had stabilized me, I called my dad and told him about the accident. I heard him curse under his breath and that made me feel even worse. I almost burst into tears, but that just wouldn't be right. I had to be strong. The images came back inconclusive. The good news was the doctors didn't see any major breaks to my spine. My pelvis was smashed and all of the ligaments around my midsection had been ripped away from my bones.

It was a long road to recovery. I promised God that if he let me walk again, I would quit riding for good.

I did, in fact, walk again at five weeks post-injury, even though the doctors told me it would be *three months* before I would be able to walk on my own and *six months* before I'd be able to ride again—if at all. The reason I recovered so quickly is because I had to. Winalota Cash was running in a set of derby trials six weeks after the injury, and if I wasn't available for the race, another jockey would gladly take my place. If that were to happen, I might have lost the mount on the greatest horse in the country — permanently. I recovered well enough to ride him (even though the pain was excruciating in that first race back) and we went on to win several more derbies together that year before I honored my deal with God. I simply should have kept my dad's words of advice and not gotten on a horse I didn't know, for a trainer who was questionable.

This life lesson has served me very well since then, mostly in the world of investing. Stay with what you understand, and avoid anything that seems rushed or makes you feel uncomfortable. And never make an investment simply because you feel bad for the person selling it.

USE IT OR LOSE IT

At this point, it seems everyone owns a smartphone, and each phone is filled with dozens or even hundreds of apps. We are all guilty of getting sucked into purchasing stuff on our phones which we don't really need. We hear about a certain app from a friend or discussed in a social media post at one time or another and so we decide we really need it, too. We sign up for the trial period just to see if we'll really like it. Stop for a second and consider how many apps you currently use on a regular basis. Now consider how many apps you have on a subscription basis in which there is a very subtle fee charged to your credit card or online account each month or each year. These sly app developers rely on our forgetfulness when they offer a *30-day free trial period*, as they know that a large percentage of people who click on their offer will forget to cancel the subscription. Make it a habit never to pay for a subscription-based service or product unless you will be a serious user who derives necessary value to offset the cost. To be certain you don't forget to cancel an unnecessary subscription, set a 25-day reminder in your calendar to *"consider cancelling the subscription for such and such app."* Additionally, go into your phone settings and review all current subscriptions to determine if they should stay or go.

Debt is like any other trap.
Easy enough to get in to
and hard enough
to get out of.

JOSH BILLINGS

CHAPTER TWELVE

DEBT

This is always a fun topic for me. I really enjoy seeing how people choose to project themselves to others. Too often, people put on a show but don't have any real assets to back up what they have. For example, we all know that family who has the latest and greatest of everything but has a near negative net worth. Back on the farm, we'd call them a*ll hat and no cattle*. A couple new cars, a boat in the garage, recreational vehicles, ever-changing wardrobes, and they eat out nearly every meal. What's on the surface is seldom what's underneath. Financing a fancy lifestyle is quite common these days. There is no wonder why we are a nation in debt. The mental math is simple. As long as the monthly payment falls in line with monthly take-home pay, the spending can continue. If you drew back the curtain to examine the financial shape of most of these people however, it would show you a completely different picture. Cars, boats, and toys all depreciate in value. They don't help build net worth, they destroy it. What we need to focus on is an affordable lifestyle in which the things obtained may be purchased within the budget and without a loan attached.

Look around and consider all of the options for your personal entertainment. There are countless ways to spend money in pursuit of contentment. This might come in the form of daily swipes to the credit or debit card for small pleasures such as a Mocha Frappuccino or convenience store goodies. It may mean bigger commitments such as buying the latest technology gadgets or an RV or ATVs. Many get addicted to the chemical endorphin delivered to the brain every time a purchase is made. They just can't stop buying. New clothes, new furniture, new cars and new toys are on the radar all of the time. This mental game is nothing but a ruse, and a very common road to financial ruin.

For those using debt to boost their future worth, I say carry on, but do so with a plan. Too many students forget just how powerful debt can be. If the debt isn't monitored, it's like getting swept up in storm while out at sea. You can't necessarily see the danger until it's too late. The dangers aren't immediately explained, so young students fresh out of college don't have any idea how their large debt levels will impact their long-term financial wellness. From my personal research, very few high school financial literacy courses are hitting the mark. Teachers do their best, but most aren't trained in how to explain the material and how to turn the information into real-life planning. It would be like me teaching aeronautics or engineering. I wouldn't have the background or experience to teach the content. We need to do a better job of properly teaching our youth about financial concepts in our country. Heavy debt, for example, often leads to a life of misery and despair.

My youngest brother, Brody, was on his way to a career in

racetrack management. He had completed his degree at the University of Arizona in their Racetrack Industry Program and in doing so, had built up a large amount of student debt. After graduation, he moved to Fort Collins, Colorado and enrolled in the MBA program at Colorado State University. Brody never mentioned to me how much debt he had incurred to get his education, but nonetheless, it began to wear on him. He was working and making decent money, but he couldn't see how on earth he would be able to pay off the $60,000+ student loan he had accumulated.

Brody was born on Christmas Eve in 1982. He grew up in a turbulent environment and his dad, Randy, never taught him how to handle money or which financial traps to watch out for. He didn't have a father figure at all. Mom left Randy for good when Brody was only 7 and about that time, I left the state to pursue my riding career, so I didn't get to spend much time with him when he was younger. After I retired from riding, Ben, Brody, and I did everything as a group. We hunted, fished, took trips together and spent every holiday in the same house. Things appeared to be fine, but they weren't.

On October 6, 2009, while on his own in Fort Collins, Brody killed himself. This tragedy happened just five days after I had left my previous broker to open my own investment firm. Brody had called me two days before and we had talked about him still needing to sign the transfer papers so he could move his Roth IRA over to my new firm. He joked that he planned to leave his account with my old firm because they had more history than I did. We ended the call laughing — just like usual. That was the last time I ever talked to my brother and I still ask myself why I didn't see what he must have been going through. He was simply overwhelmed and couldn't see a way out, yet he had too much pride to ask for help. I believe Brody would be alive today if he had understood the issues of debt better and had a clearer picture of how he would be able to pay off his student loans. I know I could have helped him come up with a plan. I simply didn't ask if he felt he was on track with his goals. It is a known fact that having a plan creates better outcomes and provides more peace of mind. With a financial plan, Brody could have begun building toward his future and would have had a better outlook on life.

I feel like I failed him. With all of the pain my whole family endured, I vowed to do something in his legacy. I don't want to see another bright young man or woman make a life-ending decision due to short-term worries. This was the main reason I created the *Livastride Foundation*. The idea was already planted in my mind, but I didn't have the inner drive to get it off the ground. With Brody's suicide, I knew it had to be done. Social media and the pressures kids face today are overwhelming. They are constantly comparing themselves to one another and trying to measure up in popularity, success, appearance, and how much fun they're having minute-to-minute. Shouldn't we do something to put our youth in the position to succeed over their lifetimes? What they need is knowledge and real-world examples of how they *can* do that.

We began ramping up the financial literacy boot camp and also created events and activities to promote interaction, fitness and living life to its fullest. For six years we hosted an annual baseball tournament for teams ranging from 8 and under all the way up to 14 and under as well as a home-run derby. Families of suicide victims would throw out the first pitch for each championship game and we spoke to the players about the devastation and destruction families face when a child takes his or her own life. I believe that our message affected a lot of kids in those moments, but the event that we are most proud of, and that we believe will offer a lifetime of benefits, is the financial boot camp.

The need for this type of learning is shocking. A recent report conducted by the Federal Government found that between 2001 and 2016, the real amount of student debt owed by American households more than tripled, from about $340 billion to more than $1.3 Trillion. Over 40 percent of Americans are struggling with their debt obligations — not to mention a basic grasp of financial literacy. A mere 28 percent of students could correctly answer three questions on inflation, interest and risk diversification. Students had a very slim understanding of their educational loans, the report also noted.[30]

WHEN IS DEBT ACCEPTABLE?

Those growing up in the baby boom generation most likely heard from their parents early and often about avoiding debt and keeping plenty of cash on hand. After all, baby boomer parents had experienced the Great Depression and the aftermath was undoubtedly life-changing. I heard about it from my grandparents who'd learned how to get by with next to nothing. Unemployment was 20 percent or higher in some places, businesses were closing down and people were losing their homes and their cars. It was real – and it happened without a precedent, so our country's leaders didn't have experience from which to draw. We eventually pulled through, but not without a few scars.

In the Great Depression, Americans dealt with poverty and eventually inflation – both of which were devastating. They learned to save money and take on little-to-no debt. Basically, they grew up with the

---

30 "Board of Governors of the Federal Reserve System." *The Fed - Student Loan Debt and Aggregate Consumption Growth,* https://www.federalreserve.gov/econres/notes/feds-notes/student-loan-debt-and-aggregate-consumption-growth-20180221.htm.

idea to *pay cash for everything and don't trust banks or investment firms.*

The *boomerang* generation of the 1980's (so named because they left home for college or to start a family, only to come circling back after losing a job or overpaying for a home which they eventually lost in the real estate collapse) has had to learn the hard way about excessive debt and its evils. It was the *me* generation. If the parents had a $300,000 home, then the kids wanted a $400,000 home. Their friends bought one without a hitch and the bank would still "give" them the money, so why wait? **NINJA** loans were the new way to achieve home ownership. **N**o **I**ncome, **N**o **J**ob, or **A**ssets – *Loan Approved.* Such was the case beginning around 2005 and accelerating into 2007.

Fast forward to 2019: Have we learned anything from the two different generations? I hope so. I hope we've learned that borrowers have to have some skin in the game and lenders need to be much more careful before doling out cash for speculative purchases. Somehow, everyone involved in real estate began assuming homes and land increased in value perpetually and never faced a decline. But now, one thing I quite often see is people swinging back too far the other direction. They are unwilling to let go of cash – afraid to invest in new ideas or businesses. Further, banks are so overly strict now on lending (mainly due to the untimely implementation of government lending regulations) that accessing capital is a tedious ordeal.

Housing speculation and excessive debt load caused the Great Recession of 2007-2009. Although scary and unsettling, it was nothing close to the level of the Great Depression of the late 1920's and early 1930's. I'll go out on a limb and predict that we will not experience a recession of that magnitude during the next 30 years. Fortunately, with the latest recession, we had hindsight as a guide so our policy-makers and federal officials acted swiftly to stimulate the economy, rescue financial institutions that were critical to the nation's survival and promote a degree of confidence in the American people. However, we still saw people tighten their belts, cancel vacations, and compete for jobs that were dwindling by the day.

What can *you* do to help our country avoid another collapse caused by excessive borrowing?

- **Lock in low rates** – Financing a home is probably about as cheap as it will be in our lifetimes. Purchasing a home is a dream for most people. The rule of thumb is to make sure you put at least 20 percent down. Thirty-year fixed loans in the 3-4 percent range will probably look like a dream a few years from now. If you haven't refinanced and your loan is at 5 percent or more, you may want to consider looking into the terms of a new loan. Then, with the savings you'll receive on your mortgage payment, fund an IRA or Roth IRA (if eligible) and invest those dollars for the long haul. It's not the best idea to pay off your mortgage at such low rates. If you can make more on your investments than the rate on your mortgage, you are money ahead.

- **Don't finance consumer debt** – Try to save up enough to buy your car or truck without using a loan. Financing a vehicle is a consumer loan and is not deductible. If you absolutely must finance a vehicle, consider utilizing a home equity line for the cash to purchase the vehicle. They are generally tax deductible, are free to establish and the rates are usually pretty reasonable. Consider getting a home equity line regardless. You don't pay any interest unless you tap it and they are easy to obtain at most banks. You never know when you may need to access capital quickly. And NEVER carry balances on a credit card. This is the number one wealth killer in our society. More to come on this one.

- **Avoid sales gimmicks** – Should you buy or lease a vehicle? I believe you should always buy. Leasing is a way for auto dealers to make more of a profit. I realize there are certain tax benefits for leasing but they don't generally pencil out after considering the payments and residual value. Plus, if you drive over the mileage limits plan on getting hammered in extra fees. Purchase a good quality vehicle in the used car lot. Look for one with low miles, good condition, and a solid reputation for longevity. You'll knock 20 percent or more off of the new car price and still have a great vehicle for years to come. Plan on driving it for 10 or more years, or for as long as you can before trading it in for another vehicle. Don't assume you should just get used to having a car payment. The goal is to not have any payments at all. The more you can avoid payments, the less you'll lose in interest charges, and in turn, the more residual cash you'll have to invest every month.

- **Talk to Ben Franklin** – If you aren't aware, Ben Franklin is the man pictured on the $100 bill. Parting with him is often hard to do. This is one reason it can be beneficial to use cash versus a credit card. Who should ever use a credit card then? Well it's like this – if you're overweight, don't pull into Dunkin' Donuts for a snack. If you have high cholesterol, don't eat bacon and egg sandwiches. If you are an uncontrolled spender, stay away from credit cards. Credit cards are a convenience item. They are valuable tools for those who can manage their spending. This absolutely means paying off the balance each month. Let me repeat – DO NOT CARRY A BALANCE ON YOUR CARD. If you don't have enough cash in the bank to pay for your card purchases, then you DON'T use it – basically, you don't buy.

    On the plus side, I love them because they provide a statement to record exactly where my money is spent, as well as providing a handy, year-end summary for tax planning purposes. Additionally, they allow users to accumulate rewards points or cash back after purchasing a certain amount on the card. They also allow us to avoid packing large sums of cash around which could be lost or stolen. If a credit card is lost or stolen, we aren't really out anything if we report it right away. Just call the credit card company or bank to report it and they will immediately cancel the card. I think keeping some cash in your pocket is a good idea. Just keep it to a reasonable level. Credit card companies have changed the landscape of consumer spending. Transactions are even secure online. Just make sure the site contains *"https"* before purchasing – the "s" stands for *secure*. I liken a credit card to a hammer. It can be a useful and helpful tool if it's in the right hands. Give a hammer to someone who doesn't know how to use it and you'll see some bloody fingers. Know who you are and stick with your strengths. If you can't be trusted with a credit card, use a debit card, which won't allow you to overspend. The downside is, they are essentially just like carrying cash. If someone steals your debit card and gets your pin, your balances are as good as gone.

■ **Just say no!** – Lending to family, friends or hard-dollar borrowers is fraught with problems – be careful here. Not only will you experience awkward family get-togethers, but you could also see no payments come in for months at a time. More times than not, we see these situations turn people against one another, and it's a quick way to lose a friend. Sometimes they work out but be sure to have the loan drawn up legally and with some compensation for late payments. Communicating and discussing expectations up front is critical. As for hard dollar loans, I don't recommend them. Most people with good credit histories can get financing through traditional banks or financing institutions. Those who are desperate will turn to this structure when nothing else is available. If you do lend money in this fashion, make sure the collateral is something you really want to own or can quickly re-sell if it comes to that. I mainly dislike the lack of liquidity and high risk with these loans.

■ **Don't buy what you can't afford!** –That sounds simplistic, but I'm quite often amazed at how much people spend, yet they have no idea how they will pay for it. If you currently have existing consumer debt for things like vehicles, appliances, furniture, clothing, boats and other toys, get busy paying it off. Start with the highest-interest rate first and do everything in your power to wipe that balance out. Then move on to the next highest-rate item. You will get dialed in and focused on paying off these debts after you see one item get eliminated. Stay with it. And stop digging yourself in deeper. If you find yourself in a hole, the first thing to do is step away from the shovel.

In summary, debt doesn't have to be a four-letter word. We can use debt to our advantage if we don't abuse it. Keeping interest rates as low as possible and avoiding penalties and fees are basic priorities. But also remember that having debt can actually allow us to use capital in other ways, hopefully to enhance our net worth. Savvy investors and executives understand this idea of compound interest and leverage. If your goal is to increase your net worth, consider keeping cash invested in higher-yielding assets than that of your debt service interest rate. This doesn't usually apply to credit card debt, as the interest rates are typically north of 15 percent and earning that type of return on investments is just not realistic. This strategy mainly applies to mortgage debt, where the rate may be 4.5 percent or lower, yet you are averaging six to 10 percent on your equity portfolio. This can allow your net worth to expand faster than if you used all of your capital to pay off the debt.

Finally, and most importantly, seek help if you are feeling overwhelmed or unsure of yourself. There are tons of wonderful financial advisors who are willing to help and most won't be looking to profit from answering some questions or providing a few specific pointers. A college or advanced degree is important, but amassing enormous debt in the pursuit of such shouldn't ruin your life – or, as in Brody's case, end it.

When in doubt, let your horse do the thinkin'.

COWBOY WISDOM

CHAPTER THIRTEEN

STAYING THE COURSE

A good coach, personal trainer, doctor, dentist or even a friend should all provide one important contribution to our well-being – keep us from doing something stupid. Coaches make us show up on time and prepare for what is to come. They teach us how to communicate and work hard to get the most out of our God-given talents. Think about any famous coach or even one you know personally. What words come to mind to describe him or her? Traits such as dedicated, honest, passionate, competitive, perceptive, intelligent or determined might be used to describe him or her. These people force us to raise the bar – to be better than we can be on our own. The same may be said of a personal trainer. They are skilled in knowing just how much we can handle both physically and mentally in order to transform our bodies and minds into better versions of ourselves.

Many people and/or professionals in various capacities are deemed important to our health and happiness. In the same way a good doctor can prolong your physical health, a good financial planner can prolong your financial health. Since money is one of the key drivers of happiness, this in turn means that a financial planner can directly impact your quality of life.

I believe the main benefits derived from having a financial advisor are:

1) They create a plan for you to reach your goals and help you to navigate life changes.

2) They help you avoid making mistakes when your emotions try to get the better of you.

An ongoing study involving psychology and investor behavior is very well known in the financial industry as the Dalbar study. Conducted every year since 1994, the study measures individual investor returns versus the returns of the unmanaged S&P 500 index. The study routinely shows that equity investors, left to their own irrational behavior, significantly underperform the stock index, which isn't affected by emotion since it remains fully invested at all times. Essentially, individual investors who don't have a professional advisor to help them will often react in the wrong way when markets become shaky. The first thing they want to do is sell out and wait for the all-clear signal. This alone is the single biggest reason the average stock-investor return from 1997 to 2017 was only 4.79 percent and yet the S&P 500 produced a 7.68 percent average return over the same period. Even more recently in 2016, the average investor realized a 7.26 percent return versus the unmanaged S&P 500 return of 11.96 percent. Even in years when markets fall, individual investors typically underperform. In 2018 the S&P 500 dropped 4.38 percent compared to the average investor losing 9.42 percent.[31] Said in another way, most investors think they are capable of doing it themselves, but the facts prove otherwise.

Yes, fees are important. I want to get the best deal I can when I'm hiring a lawn care company or a repair man. However, I have also learned the hard way that going the cheap route may backfire and cost much more in the long run than simply paying for quality work the first time. I've handled odd jobs enough to distinguish between what I should and should not do myself. Since I'm not an expert in a wide variety of tasks, I typically make several mistakes, causing me to redo what I did incorrectly the first time – more time, more equipment and more frustration. After learning this lesson the hard way, I decided to hire experienced professionals for specialized jobs which I am unqualified to perform. My stress essentially vanished and I was able to spend my time focused on the things I wanted or needed to do. For me, that usually includes spending time at my office helping my clients reach their investment objectives, hanging out with my wife and kids, trail running and going to CrossFit workouts, taking care of my horses, and coaching softball. You can come up with your list of life priorities as well.

Hiring a professional should add value without breaking the bank. The value added needs to offset the additional cost over simply going it alone. For each job or service you are considering, take out a sheet of scratch paper and make two columns. Label the first column *Pros*, and the second column *Cons*. Write down each positive (pro) and each negative (con) consideration in the respective column and assign a cost value to each line item. Total up the values in each column and then

---

[31] Szala, Ginger. "Bad Behavior Cost Equity-Fund Investors 5 Percentage Points in 2018: Dalbar." *ThinkAdvisor*, 10 Apr. 2019, https://www.thinkadvisor.com/2019/04/10/bad-behavior-cost-equity-fund-investors-5-percentage-points-in-2018-dalbar/?slreturn=20190808011440.

subtract the cons from the pros. If you end up with a positive number, it makes sense to hire someone to do the job or pay for the service. If the number is negative, do it yourself. Each potential job should be mapped out this way.

Weigh *all* of the costs, including your time and the energy necessary to do it alone. Sometimes trying to be too conservative will end up costing you in the long run. I have a couple of acquaintances who fit this bill – a brother and sister. They grew up in a cost conscious household in which their parents felt the need to do almost everything themselves. They were taught to save money and were never taught to share or to pay for outside services. Upon their parents' passing, they each inherited stock in various companies. Since they didn't see the value in having an advisor monitor those assets, they simply tucked them away in a brokerage account and left the investments unsupervised. Over a period of years, several of the companies stumbled with their business models, resulting in a steep drop in the share prices. The two lost tens of thousands in values yet did nothing, and to this day continue with the supposedly cheaper route of not hiring a financial advisor.

So, you may be asking yourself, *"What is a financial advisor worth?"* Vanguard actually did a very in-depth study on this question to determine if hiring a financial advisor made a positive impact on investor returns. They broke down the various roles and services that a financial advisor *should* provide. (There is no debating that some advisors are better than others. This study is based on assessed alpha, positive contributions, for each of the financial advisory functions from a skilled and competent advisor.) Vanguard determined that there are seven broadly defined advisory roles:

1) Suitable asset allocation using broadly diversified funds/ETF's
2) Cost-effective implementation (low expense ratios)
3) Rebalancing
4) Behavioral coaching
5) Asset allocation adjustment based on economic cycle and financial conditions
6) Spending strategy (withdrawal plan)
7) Assembling a total-return portfolio versus income-only investing

For each role, a fee was assessed based on value added according to the study. The largest annual fee weighting at 1.15 percent was assigned to No. 4 – Behavioral Coaching. This is not surprising. As I've mentioned numerous times, investors are almost always their own worst enemy. In total, Vanguard assigned an approximate annual value of 3 percent for financial advisory services from a skilled advisor.[32] Most advisors, however, charge only a fraction of that.

From my experience, very few people have the discipline to become successful investors, which is the biggest reason I chose to write this book. People need help staying on track. It's no coincidence that consulting, therapy and personal coaching are some of the fastest growing professions in our society. There are strength coaches, nutrition coaches, relationship coaches, career coaches, and the list goes on for a mile and a half. These days, people don't seem to have sufficient motivation to take action on their own, nor the tenacity to stick with a written goal-plan long enough for the ink to dry. Discipline and perseverance are two characteristics which are hard to find in this era of discontent. We pay for all types of services to improve various

---

[32] "Quantifying Your Value To Your Clients." *The Vanguard Group, Inc,* https://advisors.vanguard.com/iwe/pdf/FASQAAAB.pdf

elements in our lives. We pay for golf-swing coaching, hairstyling, wardrobe shopping, grocery delivery, and a whole host of instructional programs for our kids to be better in their activities. Yet many never even consider their retirement and investment strategy, or simply feel they can handle their financial plan on their own.

I've seen up-close how that typically works out. It doesn't get off the ground. Where should financial freedom rank in your list of items worth spending money on? Would you perform your own appendectomy? Of course not. Nobody would. In our society, people can't even take care of their own headache or stuffy nose. Most people don't bat an eye when it comes to paying for what they perceive as necessary healthcare expenses. I would only hope that these same people will see the benefits in applying similar behavior with investment services. Helping people establish their own unique plan and marking the progress toward those long-term goals are definite value adds from a competent advisor.

When you begin to seriously consider your financial goals, you will find it to be an enlightening experience. Most people spend more time on their one-week family vacation plans than they do preparing for their 30 or more retirement years. There are short-term and long-term goals, small goals and ambitious goals. They are all important. You need to assign a priority level to each of your goals. I like to assign a ranking to each and then designate a probability of success, as well. If a higher-ranking goal slips below an 85 percent success likelihood, the best solution would be to pull resources from one or more lower-priority goals in order to perk up the more important targets. In this way, your goals will begin to be seen in a more realistic light.

If you remember anything from this book, I hope it is that you can change the trajectory of your life by doing something today that is really quite simple. From my perspective, building a business, writing a book, running a 100-miler and starving yourself day after day to perform your job are difficult. Investing and developing smart financial habits isn't. It's frankly a matter of taking a few small steps to get your money working as hard as you do, and sacrificing short-term spending in place of long-term financial freedom.

Dear Past, thank you for all the lessons.
Dear Future, I am now Ready!

WISE MAN

The path to becoming a millionaire isn't just for the lucky. It's for you!

BILLY PETERSON'S GALLERY

Billy, age 2 prior to first surgery.

Billy and his mother, Larie.

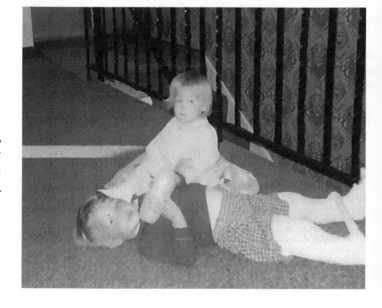

Billy, age 3, in full-body cast with his cousin.

Billy, in a full-body cast, with his sister, Kacey, ages 3 and 5.

Billy and Ben, ages 10 and 5, riding their ponies *Buckles and Cloud.*

Father Spencer and Billy, age 13, holding a 2-year-old filly.

Billy, age 14, with one of his all-time favorite horses – *Kacey's Shadow Rocket*.
Billy and his sister, Kacey, both did some great things on this horse.
Kacey won *the National High School Rodeo Queen Contest* with him.

Billy, age 11, competing in bareback riding at Junior Rodeo.

First "unofficial" race win, age 15.

First "unofficial" Thoroughbred race win, age 15.

First "official" win — Rogo Le'Blurr Wyoming Downs 1991
Horse owned by Billy's father, Spencer Peterson.

Billy on Winalota Cash in the 1995 All-American Futurity.

Billy on Winalota Cash after their victory in the All-American Futurity.

Heading into the winner's circle after the All-American.

Texas Classic Futurity Grade 1 1995.

First win at Santa Anita Park with Chief Charley in 1996.

Billy riding future world champion Sign It Super for legendary trainer Blane Schvaneveldt.

First win at Fairplex Park (Pomona) with Heaven Sent in 1996.

First win at Del Mar with Macho Bronco in 1996.

Ben, Brody, Kacey, Spencer and Billy in Ruidoso Downs winner cirlce after Spencer's horse won the Ruidoso Futurity in 2006.

Brody, Ben and Billy in 2009.

Ben and Billy,
Los Alamitos
Racecourse -
2018.

Billy and his wife, Heather, at the Canterbury Racetrack - 2019.

Billy with his family in Boston - 2018.

FINANCIAL VOCABULARY

American Depositary Receipt (ADR) – A negotiable certificate issued by a U.S. depository bank representing a specified number of shares—or as little as one share—investment in a foreign company's stock. The ADR trades on markets in the U.S. as any stock would trade.

Basis Point – Basis points, otherwise known as bps or "bips," are a unit of measure used in finance to describe the percentage change in the value or rate of a financial instrument. One basis point is equivalent to 0.01 percent (1/100th of a percent) or 0.0001 in decimal form. Likewise, a fractional basis point such as 1.5 basis points is equivalent to 0.015 percent or 0.00015 in decimal form. In most cases, basis points refer to changes in interest rates and bond yields.

Bear Market – A condition in which securities prices fall 20 percent or more from recent highs amid widespread pessimism and negative investor sentiment. Typically, bear markets are associated with declines in an overall market or index like the S&P 500, but individual securities or commodities can be considered to be in a bear market if they experience a decline of 20 percent or more over a sustained period of time - typically two months or more.

Blue Chip – A nationally recognized, well-established, and financially sound company. Blue chips generally sell high-quality, widely accepted products and services. Blue chip companies are known to weather downturns and operate profitably in the face of adverse economic conditions, which helps to contribute to their long record of stable and reliable growth.

Bull Market – The condition of a financial market of a group of securities in which prices are rising or are expected to rise. The term "bull market" is most often used to refer to the stock market but can be applied to anything that is traded, such as bonds, real estate, currencies and commodities. Because prices of securities rise and fall essentially continuously during trading, the term "bull market" is typically reserved for extended periods in which a large portion of security prices are rising. Bull markets tend to last for months or even years.

Dividend – The distribution of reward from a portion of the company's earnings and is paid to a class of its shareholders. Dividends are decided and managed by the company's board of directors, though they must be approved by the shareholders through their voting rights. Dividends can be issued as cash payments, as shares of stock, or other property, though cash dividends are the most common. Along with companies, various mutual funds and exchange traded funds (ETFs) also pay dividends.

Dove – A dove is an economic policy advisor who promotes monetary policies that usually involve low interest rates. Doves tend to support low interest rates and an expansionary monetary policy because they value indicators like low unemployment over keeping inflation low. If an economist suggests that inflation has few negative effects or calls for quantitative easing, then he or she is often called a dove or labeled as dovish.

Dow Jones Industrial Average (DJIA) – An index that tracks **30** large, publicly-owned companies trading on the New York Stock Exchange (NYSE) and the NASDAQ. The DJIA is named after Charles Dow, who created it in 1896, and his business partner, Edward Jones. Often referred to as "the Dow," the DJIA is one of the oldest, single most-watched indices in the world and includes companies such as the Walt Disney Company, Exxon Mobil Corporation and Microsoft Corporation. When the TV networks say "the market is up today," they are generally referring to the Dow.

Federal Reserve System (FRS) – The central bank of the United States. The Fed, as it is commonly known, regulates the U.S. monetary and financial system. The Federal Reserve System is composed of a central governmental agency in Washington, D.C., the Board of Governors, and 12 regional Federal Reserve Banks in major cities throughout the United States.

Gross Domestic Product (GDP) – The total monetary or market value of all the finished goods and services produced within a country's borders in a specific time period. As a broad measure of overall domestic production, it functions as a comprehensive scorecard of the country's economic health.

Hawk – A hawk, also known as an inflation hawk, is a policymaker or advisor who is predominantly concerned with interest rates as they relate to fiscal policy. A hawk generally favors relatively high interest rates in order to keep inflation in check. In other words, hawks are less concerned with economic growth than they are with recessionary pressure brought to bear by high inflation rates.

Inflation – A quantitative measure of the rate at which the average price level of a basket of selected goods and services in an economy increases over a period of time. It is the constant rise in the general level of prices where a unit of currency buys less than it did in prior periods. Often expressed as a percentage, inflation indicates a decrease in the purchasing power of a nation's currency.

Municipal Bond Fund – Fund that invests in municipal bonds. Municipal bond funds can be managed with varying objectives that are often based on location, credit quality and duration. Municipal bonds are debt securities issued by a state, municipality, county, or special purpose district (such as a public school or airport) to finance capital expenditures. Municipal bond funds are exempt from federal tax and may also be exempt from state taxes.

NASDAQ – A global electronic marketplace for buying and selling securities, as well as the benchmark index for U.S. technology stocks. NASDAQ was created by the National Association of Securities Dealers (NASD) to enable investors to trade securities on a computerized, speedy and transparent system, and commenced operations on February 8, 1971. The term, "Nasdaq" is also used to refer to the Nasdaq Composite, an index of more than 3,000 stocks listed on the NASDAQ exchange that includes the world's foremost technology and biotech giants such as Apple, Google, Microsoft, Oracle, Amazon, and Intel.

New York Stock Exchange (NYSE) – A stock exchange located in New York City that is considered the largest equities-based exchange in the world, based on the total market capitalization of its listed securities. Formerly run as a private organization, the NYSE became a public entity in 2005 following the acquisition of electronic trading exchange Archipelago. In 2007 a merger with Euronext, the largest stock exchange in Europe, led to the creation of NYSE Euronext, which was later acquired by Intercontinental Exchange, the current parent of the New York Stock Exchange.

Penny Stock – Refers to a small company's stock that typically trades for less than $5 per share. Although some penny stocks trade on large exchanges such as the New York Stock Exchange (NYSE), most penny stocks trade via over the counter (OTC) transactions.

Portfolio – A grouping of financial assets such as stocks, bonds, commodities, currencies and cash equivalents, as well as their fund counterparts, including mutual, exchange-traded and closed funds. A portfolio can also consist of non-publicly tradable securities, like real estate, art, and private investments.

Price-to-Earnings Ratio (P/E Ratio) – The ratio for valuing a company that measures its current share price relative to its per-share earnings (EPS). The price-to-earnings ratio is also sometimes known as the price multiple or the earnings multiple.

Quote – The last price at which a security or commodity traded, meaning the most recent price to which a buyer and seller agreed and at which some amount of the asset was transacted. The bid or ask quotes are the most current prices and quantities at which the shares can be bought or sold. The bid quote shows the price and quantity of which a current buyer is willing to purchase the shares, while the ask shows what a current participant is willing to sell the shares for. A quote is also referred to as an asset's "quoted price."

Real Estate Investment Trust (REIT) – Allows individual investors to buy shares in commercial real estate portfolios that receive income from a variety of properties. Properties included in a REIT portfolio may include apartment complexes, data centers, health care facilities, hotels, infrastructure—in the form of fiber cables, cell towers, and energy pipelines—office buildings, retail centers, self-storage, timberland, and warehouses.

Recession – A recession is a macroeconomic term that refers to a significant decline in general economic activity in a region, country, or the entire world that goes on for more than a few months. It is visible in industrial production, employment, real income, and wholesale-retail trade. The technical definition of a recession is two consecutive quarters of negative economic growth as measured by a country's gross domestic product (GDP), although the National Bureau of Economic Research (NBER) does not necessarily need to see this occur to call a recession.

Roth Individual Retirement Account (IRA) – Funded with after-tax dollars; the contributions are not tax deductible—but once you start withdrawing funds, qualified distributions are tax-free. These accounts are best utilized for long-term retirement assets since the compounded growth is all free of tax.

Russell 2000 Index – An index measuring the performance of approximately 2,000 smallest-cap American companies in the Russell 3000 Index, which is made up of 3,000 of the largest U.S. stocks. It is a market-cap weighted index.

Securities and Exchange Commission (SEC) – An independent federal government agency responsible for protecting investors, maintaining fair and orderly functioning of the securities markets, and facilitating capital formation. It was created by Congress in 1934 as the first federal regulator of the securities markets. The SEC promotes full public disclosure, protects investors against fraudulent and manipulative practices in the market, and monitors corporate takeover actions in the United States.

Short Sale – A short sale is the sale of an asset or stock the seller does not own. It is generally a transaction in which an investor sells borrowed securities in anticipation of a price decline; the seller is then required to return an equal number of shares at some point in the future. In contrast, a seller owns the security or stock in a long position.

Speculation – Refers to the act of conducting a financial transaction that has substantial risk of losing value but also holds the expectation of a significant gain or other major value. With speculation, the risk of loss is more than offset by the possibility of a substantial gain or other recompense.

Standard & Poor's (S&P) – A leading index provider and data source of independent credit ratings. It is also the provider of the popular S&P 500 Index. S&P was founded in 1860, offering financial market intelligence.

S&P 500 Index – The S&P 500 or Standard & Poor's 500 Index is a market-capitalization-weighted index of the 500 largest U.S. publicly traded companies. The index is widely regarded as the best gauge of large-cap U.S. equities. Other common U.S. stock market benchmarks include the Dow Jones Industrial Average or Dow 30 and the Russell 2000 Index, which represents the small-cap index.

Ticker – A ticker symbol is an arrangement of characters—usually letters—representing particular securities listed on an exchange or otherwise traded publicly. When a company issues securities to the public marketplace, it selects an available ticker symbol for its securities that investors and traders use to transact orders. Every listed security has a unique ticker symbol, facilitating the vast array of trade orders that flow through the financial markets every day.

Traditional Individual Retirement Account (IRA) – Allows individuals to direct pre-tax income toward investments that can grow tax-deferred. The IRS assesses no capital gains or dividend income taxes until the beneficiary makes a withdrawal. Individual taxpayers can contribute 100 percent of any earned compensation up to a specified maximum dollar amount. Income thresholds may also apply. Contributions to a traditional IRA may be tax-deductible depending on the taxpayer's income, tax-filing status and other factors.

Yield – Refers to the earnings generated and realized on an investment over a particular period of time, and is expressed in terms of percentage based on the invested amount or on the current market value or on the face value of the security. It includes the interest earned or dividends received from holding a particular security. Depending on the nature and valuation (fixed/fluctuating) of the security, yields may be classified as known or anticipated.

Yield to Maturity (YTM) – The total return anticipated on a bond if the bond is held until it matures. Yield to maturity is considered a long-term bond yield but it is expressed as an annual rate. In other words, it is the internal rate of return (IRR) of an investment in a bond if the investor holds the bond until maturity, with all payments made as scheduled and reinvested at the same rate. Yield to maturity is also referred to as "book yield" or "redemption yield."

FINANCIAL DISCLOSURES

This book endeavors to expand the scope of readers' financial literacy, however, it is not intended to provide investment, tax, legal, risk management, or accounting advice, and is for educational purposes only. The content is believed to be accurate but is without warranty. Readers should consult their investment, tax, legal, risk management, and accounting advisors before engaging in any transaction or strategy.

Investing always involves risk and you may incur a profit or loss. Keep mind that past performance does not guarantee future results. Rates and returns found in this book are not guaranteed and are for illustrative purposes only. There is no assurance any of the trends mentioned will continue or forecasts will occur.

The information contained in this book does not purport to be a complete description of the securities, markets, or developments referred to in this material. Any opinions stated are those of the author and not necessarily those of Raymond James. Raymond James is not affiliated with any of the companies or organizations mentioned herein. The information has been obtained from sources considered to be reliable, but we do not guarantee that the foregoing material is accurate or complete. Any information is not a complete summary or statement of all available data necessary for making an investment decision and does not constitute a recommendation to buy or sell any security. Scenarios described are hypothetical and provided for illustrative purposes only. Hypothetical examples do not represent real returns of an actual investor or investment. These calculations are hypothetical in nature, are used for illustrative purposes, and do not represent the performance of any specific investment or product. Future performance cannot be guaranteed and investment yields will fluctuate with market conditions. Rates of return will vary over time, particularly for long-term investments. Actual investor results will vary. The client experiences described may not be representative of any future experience of our clients. Keep in mind that indexes are unmanaged and individuals cannot invest directly in any index. Index performance does not include transaction costs or other fees, which will affect the actual investment performance. Individual investor results will vary. Diversification and strategic asset allocation do not ensure a profit or protect against a loss. As always with IPOs, the date of the offering is an estimate and subject to change. Please consider the potential risks involved before investing in IPOs. Dividends are not guaranteed and a company's future ability to pay dividends may be limited. Past performance may not be indicative of future results. . Dollar-cost averaging cannot guarantee a profit or protect against a loss, and you should consider your financial ability to continue purchases through periods of low price levels. Holding stocks for the long-term does not insure a profitable outcome. Rebalancing a non-retirement account could be a taxable event that may increase your tax liability. No investment strategy can guarantee success.

Please note, changes in tax laws or regulations may occur at any time and could substantially impact your situation. Raymond James financial advisors do not render advice on tax or legal matters. You should discuss any tax or legal matters with the appropriate professional.

Links are being provided for information purposes only. Raymond James is not affiliated with and does not endorse, authorize or sponsor any of the listed web sites or their respective sponsors. Raymond James is not responsible for the content of any web site or the collection or use of information regarding any web site's users and/or members.

401(k) plans are long-term retirement savings vehicles. Withdrawal of pre-tax contributions and/or earnings will be subject to ordinary income tax and, if taken prior to age 59 1/2, may be subject to a 10% federal tax penalty. Contributions to a Roth 401(k) are never tax deductible, but if certain conditions are met, distributions will be completely income tax free. Unlike Roth IRAs, Roth 401(k) participants are subject to required minimum distributions at age 70.5. Matching contributions from your employer may be subject to a vesting schedule. Contributions to a traditional IRA may be tax-deductible depending on the taxpayer's income, tax-filing status, and other factors. Withdrawal of pre-tax contributions and/or earnings will be subject to ordinary income tax and, if taken prior to age 59 1/2, may be subject to a 10% federal tax penalty. Like Traditional IRAs, contribution limits apply to Roth IRAs. In addition, with a Roth IRA, your allowable contribution may be reduced or eliminated if your annual income exceeds certain limits. Contributions to a Roth IRA are never tax deductible. Roth IRA owners must be 59½ or older and have held the IRA for five years before tax-free withdrawals are permitted.

As with other investments, there are generally fees and expenses associated with participation in a 529 plan. There is also a risk that these plans may lose money or not perform well enough to cover college costs as anticipated. Most states offer their own 529 programs, which may provide advantages and benefits exclusively for their residents. Investors should consider, before investing, whether the investor's or the designated beneficiary's home state offers any tax or other benefits that are only available for investment in such state's 529 college savings plan. Such benefits include financial aid, scholarship funds, and protection from creditors. The tax implications can vary significantly from state to state.

Investors should carefully consider the investment objectives, risks, charges and expenses associated with 529 plans before investing. This and other information about 529 plans is available in the issuer's official statement and should be read carefully before investing. Investors should consult a tax advisor about any state tax consequences of an investment in a 529 plan.

Variable annuities are long term investments and optional riders carry additional fees and charges. Early withdrawals prior to 59 ½ years incur a 10% tax penalty. While there is no risk to the original principal if the annuitant/owner (varies by contract) should die during the accumulation period, both the investment return and principal value of variable annuities will fluctuate in response to changing market conditions. Guarantees are based on the claims paying ability of the insurer. An investment in the securities underlying variable annuities involves investment risk, including possible loss of principal. The contract, when redeemed, may be worth more or less than the total amount invested. Past performance is no guarantee of future results.

A fixed annuity is a long-term, tax-deferred insurance contract designed for retirement. It allows you to create a fixed stream of income through a process called annuitization and also provides a fixed rate of return based on the terms of the contract. Fixed annuities have limitations. If you decide to take your money out early, you may face fees called surrender charges. Plus, if you're not yet 59½, you may also have to pay an additional 10% tax penalty on top of ordinary income taxes. You should also know that a fixed annuity contains guarantees and protections that are subject to the issuing insurance company's ability to pay for them.

Real estate investments can be subject to different and greater risks than more diversified investments. Declines in the value of real estate, economic conditions, property taxes, tax laws and interest rates all present potential risks to real estate investments. Raymond James Financial Advisor do not solicit or offer residential mortgage products and are unable to accept any residential mortgage loan applications or to offer or negotiate terms of any such loan. You will be referred to a qualified Raymond James Bank employee for your residential mortgage lending needs.

ETF shareholders should be aware that the general level of stock or bond prices may decline, thus affecting the value of an exchange-traded fund. Although exchange-traded funds are designed to provide investment results that generally correspond to the price and yield performance of their respective underlying indexes, the funds may not be able to exactly replicate the performance of the indexes because of fund expenses and other factors.

Investors should consider the investment objectives, risks, charges and expenses of an exchange traded product carefully before investing. The prospectus contains this and other information and should be read carefully before investing. The prospectus is available from your investment professional.

Bond prices and yields are subject to change based upon market conditions and availability. If bonds are sold prior to maturity, you may receive more or less than your initial investment. There is an inverse relationship between interest rate movements and fixed income prices. Generally, when interest rates rise, fixed income prices fall and when interest rates fall, fixed income prices rise.

High-yield bonds are not suitable for all investors. The risk of default may increase due to changes in the issuer's credit quality. Price changes may occur due to changes in interest rates and the liquidity of the bond. When appropriate, these bonds should only comprise a modest portion of a portfolio.

Investments in municipal securities may not be appropriate for all investors, particularly those who do not stand to benefit from the tax status of the investment. Municipal bond interest is not subject to federal income tax but may be subject to AMT, state or local taxes.

Investing in commodities is generally considered speculative because of the significant potential for investment loss. Their markets are likely to be volatile and there may be sharp price fluctuations even during periods when prices overall are rising. Prior to making an investment decision, please consult with your financial advisor about your individual situation.

Every type of investment, including mutual funds, involves risk. Risk refers to the possibility that you will lose money (both principal and any earnings) or fail to make money on an investment. Changing market conditions can create fluctuations in the value of a mutual fund investment. In addition, there are fees and expenses associated with investing in mutual funds that do not usually occur when purchasing individual securities directly.

Investors should carefully consider the investment objectives, risks, charges and expenses of mutual funds. The prospectus contains this and other information about mutual funds. The prospectus is available from our office [or from the fund company] and should be read carefully.

Sector investments are companies engaged in business related to a specific sector. They are subject to fierce competition and their products and services may be subject to rapid obsolescence. There are additional risks associated with investing in an individual sector, including limited diversification. Investing in small cap stocks generally involves greater risks, and therefore, may not be appropriate for every investor. The prices of small company stocks may be subject to more volatility than those of large company stocks.

International investing involves special risks, including currency fluctuations, differing financial accounting standards, and possible political and economic volatility. Investing in emerging markets can be riskier than investing in well-established foreign markets. Investing involves risk and investors may incur a profit or a loss.

Sustainable/Socially Responsible Investing (SRI) considers qualitative environmental, social and corporate governance, also known as ESG criteria, which may be subjective in nature. There are additional risks associated with Sustainable/Socially Responsible Investing (SRI), including limited diversification and the potential for increased volatility. There is no guarantee that SRI products or strategies will produce returns similar to traditional investments. Because SRI criteria exclude certain securities/products for non-financial reasons, investors may forego some market opportunities available to those who do not use these criteria. Investors should consult their investment professional prior to making an investment decision.

Bitcoin issuers are not registered with the SEC, and the bitcoin marketplace is currently unregulated. Bitcoin and other cryptocurrencies are a very speculative investment and involves a high degree of risk.

Indices are not available for direct investment. Any investor who attempts to mimic the performance of an index would incur fees and expenses which would reduce returns. The S&P 500 is an unmanaged index of 500 widely held stocks that is generally considered representative of the U.S. stock market. The Dow Jones Industrial Average (DJIA), commonly known as "The Dow" is an index representing 30 stock of companies maintained and reviewed by the editors of the Wall Street Journal.

This information is not intended as a solicitation or an offer to buy or sell any company or security referred to herein. Raymond James may make a market in any of the securities mentioned herein. Every investor's situation is unique and you should consider your investment goals, risk tolerance and time horizon before making any investment. Prior to making an investment decision, please consult with your financial advisor about your individual situation.

Certified Financial Planner Board of Standards Inc. (CFP Board) owns the certification marks CFP®, CERTIFIED FINANCIAL PLANNER™, CFP® (with plaque design), and CFP® (with flame design) in the U.S., which it authorizes use of by individuals who successfully complete CFP Board's initial and ongoing certification requirements.

Made in the USA
San Bernardino,
CA